PRAISE FOR MINDFUL CLASSROOMS™

"*Mindful Classrooms* offers wonderfully concrete activities for teachers who want to lead mindful movement and breathing exercises with their students in the classroom. It's the perfect complement to the daily guided sitting practices that more and more schools are embedding into the school day to benefit both students and teachers. This book can help educators foster a more mindful classroom in which to support their students' social and emotional learning."

—Laurie Grossman, director of social justice and educational equity, Inner Explorer, Inc.

"I have been inspired by the research presented that shows the positive effects of secular mindfulness in schools. It allows time for reflection while reducing stress and anxiety. Learning how to relax and concentrate on the task at hand is important and worthwhile for students, teachers, and even superintendents. I'm hopeful for *Mindful Classrooms*, and I want to encourage everyone to reflect on the importance of having a proper balance."

—Dr. Paul Cruz, Austin ISD superintendent

"*Mindful Classrooms* has helped teach our students and staff to self-regulate when they are frustrated, angry, or anxious, or they need a brain break. Academics are very important but with the help of *Mindful Classrooms*, we are teaching whole-child life skills that will complement their academic work."

—Mark Overly, Carrcroft Elementary principal

"My students have been more aware of themselves and how their attitude affects themselves and others. They've even told me 'I was able to do this when I was angry, and I wanted to yell but I just breathed, and I worked through it.'"

—Callie Alldredge, Pflugerville Elementary third-grade teacher

"Students and teachers quickly embraced using *Mindful Classrooms* on a daily basis. Both groups stated it helps them be more centered and focused. It's had a positive impact on my campus from kindergarten through fifth grade."

—Genia Antoine, Pflugerville Elementary principal

"One of my favorite parts of the day is walking into a classroom where the teacher is leading a mindfulness activity. Seeing a room full of kiddos, sitting on the carpet, working on their breathing together, with the teacher modeling it with them . . . it's really amazing to see. The *Mindful Classrooms* activities have been huge for our campus climate and we have even started incorporating mindfulness at our morning assemblies. It's that important."

—Brian Hill, Pillow Elementary principal

"I have experienced *Mindful Classrooms* as both a parent and an educator. Both my son and my students alike have learned how to use mindfulness as a tool to self-regulate. Professionally and personally I have learned how to use mindfulness as a way to manage everyday stressors that come along with being an educator, a wife, and a mother."

—Allison Hinojosa, Gullett Elementary preK teacher and mom

MINDFUL CLASSROOMS™

Daily 5-Minute Practices to Support Social-Emotional Learning (PreK to Grade 5)

James Butler, M.Ed.

free spirit
PUBLISHING®

Library of Congress Cataloging-in-Publication Data
Names: Butler, James, author.
Title: Mindful classrooms : daily 5-minute practices to support social-emotional learning (PreK to grade 5) / James Butler, M.Ed.
Description: Minneapolis, MN : Free Spirit Publishing, [2019] | Includes bibliographical references and index.
Identifiers: LCCN 2018045879 (print) | LCCN 2018055433 (ebook) | ISBN 9781631983702 (Web PDF) | ISBN 9781631983719 (ePub) | ISBN 9781631983696 (pbk.) | ISBN 1631983695 (pbk.)
Subjects: LCSH: Affective education. | Mindfulness (Psychology) | Emotions and cognition. | Emotional intelligence—Study and teaching (Preschool) | Emotional intelligence—Study and teaching (Elementary)
Classification: LCC LB1072 (ebook) | LCC LB1072 .B88 2019 (print) | DDC 370.15/34—dc23
LC record available at https://lccn.loc.gov/2018045879

Free Spirit Publishing does not have control over or assume responsibility for author or third-party websites and their content. At the time of this book's publication, all facts and figures cited within are the most current available. All telephone numbers, addresses, and website URLs are accurate and active; all publications, organizations, websites, and other resources exist as described in this book; and all have been verified as of February 2021. If you find an error or believe that a resource listed here is not as described, please contact Free Spirit Publishing.

Original photography by Stephanie Friedman Photography, used with permission
Logo design: Bryony Gomez-Palacio, Under Consideration, LLC

Edited by Brian Farrey-Latz
Cover and interior design by Shannon Pourciau

10 9 8 7 6 5 4 3
Printed in the United States of America

Free Spirit Publishing Inc.
6325 Sandburg Road, Suite 100
Minneapolis, MN 55427-3674
(612) 338-2068
help4kids@freespirit.com
freespirit.com

FSC
www.fsc.org
MIX
Paper from responsible sources
FSC® C005010

Free Spirit offers competitive pricing.
Contact edsales@freespirit.com for pricing information on multiple quantity purchases.

Dedication

My amazing partner, Lindsey Wineholt, for her never-ending support and timely reminders for me to do some mindful breathing.

The students, families, and staff at Mangetti Combined School (Namibia); Winn Elementary, T.A. Brown Elementary, Barbara Jordan Elementary, and Gullett Elementary (Austin, TX) for allowing me to grow, become the best teacher I can be, and support my whole-child education beliefs.

The incredibly generous 274 friends, family members, coworkers, and strangers who pledged to support the original Mindful Classrooms Kickstarter project. This book is possible because of each one of y'all.

CONTENTS

The following scripts and modifications are available to download.
Please see page 181 for instructions.

INTRODUCTION

As an educator, you know that teaching kids social-emotional and self-regulation skills should be "is" important for their development. But with more emphasis on testing and academics, it's rare when schools set aside time for teachers to instruct their students in the use of these important tools. An ideal solution is to find short but effective lessons that fit easily into existing curricula. Mindfulness provides that solution.

The Basics of Mindfulness

You may have heard the term *mindfulness* in the news or during professional development. It's quickly gaining traction in the education world for its simplicity and usefulness. As defined by Jon Kabat-Zinn, a professor of medicine at the University of Massachusetts Medical School and creator of mindfulness-based stress reduction (MBSR), mindfulness is "paying attention in a particular way: on purpose, in the present moment, and nonjudgmentally."

Put another way, mindfulness is a means to center your focus on a singular task (breathing, eating, listening) that clears your mind of all other thoughts. As adults, our minds are always racing. We're thinking about having to go to the dentist after work and walking the dog and the important meeting we have to prepare for in two weeks. We also spend lots of time thinking about how embarrassing it was when we were late to the staff meeting or how we argued with our mother on the phone. Our brains get crowded with all these thoughts—past and future—which can lead to stress.

What we sometimes forget is that kids can feel this stress too. Their brains are also buzzing with worries about the past and future, which can make it hard for them to focus on what's happening in class or keep their emotions in check.

Mindfulness practices offer simple and efficient techniques to bring one's attention to the present moment. In doing so—when we temporarily release our worries about the future and past—we free up space in our minds for the here and now and charge up our abilities to concentrate. The best part is mindfulness doesn't require hours and hours. A successful mindfulness practice takes just a few minutes a day.

Like most things, a mindfulness practice requires . . . well, practice. To reap the benefits, it's important that the techniques are performed regularly, daily if possible. The more you do them, the easier they become. Starting a mindfulness practice can be difficult. Frequently, when new practitioners begin, they find their attention pulled away by stray thoughts while trying to focus on something like breathing. As a result, they get disappointed and give up quickly. This is where the "nonjudgmental" part of Kabat-Zinn's definition comes in.

It's important, when crafting a mindfulness practice, to accept errors and move on. Let's say you're spending a minute focusing on your breathing. You're doing well for about ten seconds and then you remember you must buy your cousin a birthday present. This is *going* to happen. It's how our brains have been conditioned. Mindfulness encourages you to recognize that this thought happened, accept it, push it out of your mind, and pick up where you left off by focusing on your breath again. No blaming. No disappointment. Just acceptance. With diligence, practitioners find themselves able to go longer periods of time staying focused on their breathing. It becomes much easier not to be distracted by other thoughts.

By allowing yourself to periodically live in the moment and clear your mind of other thoughts, you can gain clarity, calm, and empathy.

And this is what we want to do for students. We want to give them the tools that help them channel their focus, practice compassion and empathy, and self-regulate their emotions.

About This Book

In 2002, I started teaching kindergarten and prekindergarten in Austin, Texas. My teaching philosophy was always centered around compassion for my students and their families. But it's one thing to show and believe in compassion and another thing to integrate those ideals into a classroom with guidance. I would have greatly benefited from some concrete exercises that supported social and emotional learning. What I didn't realize at the time was that I already had the tools I needed to create those exercises.

I had been familiar with the concept of mindfulness for some time and had used various techniques to help me handle how overwhelmed I felt, both professionally and personally. I quickly saw how spending just a few minutes a day concentrating on my breath could help me calm down and focus on the matters at hand. It was a life changer. But I hadn't yet discovered how these techniques might have applications in the classroom.

In 2009, I volunteered as a high school English and math teacher in Namibia. The conditions there were often harsh and, as a result, my students had overwhelming needs. I began using mindfulness in my classroom to help them (and myself) cope with adversities. This is where I really began to understand how these techniques could be a positive influence in school for students and teachers.

When I returned to Austin in 2010 to teach again, I began dealing with depression and anxiety, so I sought help. In therapy, I learned more specifics about mindfulness. Through a simple five-minute daily mindfulness practice, I was able to be present for everyone in my classroom. More than that, my practice helped me prevent my personal life from getting in the way of how I interacted with my students.

I was able to get to the root of their behavior rather than just deal with the behavior itself. My mindfulness practice also helped me recognize any biases or preconceived notions that I had about my students and how those notions might have been impacting how I was treating them. Overall, I became more compassionate in my instruction and more focused on my students' social and emotional growth.

I introduced mindfulness techniques to my classroom. The consistency of daily breathing was incredibly helpful in developing a sense of routine for my kindergarten students at a Title I school. I saw an increase in self-awareness and self-management, which led to improved responsible decision-making and social awareness. Students became more considerate toward one another, exhibited more patience, and made better choices. Mindfulness helped my students deal with difficulties they were having at school, and parents reported improved behavior at home as well. I tried the daily practice at a preK classroom in a non–Title I school and saw similar results. The Austin Independent School District noted the impact my efforts were having and asked me to implement my work district-wide. Currently, I am their SEL mindfulness specialist.

As of this writing, *Mindful Classrooms* is being used in over a thousand classrooms across the United States. Even with that kind of reach, more solid evidence is required to convince some school districts and administrators to adopt new practices. Which brings us to the scientific research behind mindfulness.

Research About the Benefits of Mindfulness

The last time one of your students was angry and needed to calm down, you probably suggested that he or she stop and take a breath. Breathing is one of the oldest and best-known methods for helping someone regain control and avoid having a complete meltdown. And most of the time, breathing works. Why? It's not just a diversion. It also involves physiology and brain chemistry.

Although mindfulness entails many aspects (stretching, listening, seeing, and eating, all of which we'll discuss throughout this book), much of it revolves around breathing and focusing on breath. It's not a coincidence that this central tenet is also a popular tool when it comes to anger management. Minute by minute, breathing affects our bodies in ways we rarely think about. This is a key element of the science behind mindfulness and what it does for us.

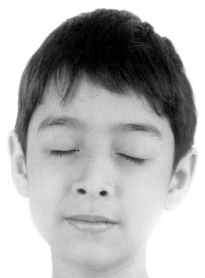

We've been taught the basics of breathing: every inhale brings nourishing oxygen to our blood and every exhale expels carbon dioxide. But the benefits don't stop there. Breathing has been shown to have positive influence on respiratory muscle activity, heart rate variability, and blood flow dynamics. Consequently, there's a notable elevation in mood, release of tension, and pain relief.

Researchers have been testing the impact of mindfulness, and the initial data is very encouraging. Neurologists, in particular, have noted the effects meditation can have on the brain.

A study published in *Trends in Cognitive Sciences* showed that the amygdala—the part of the brain that fuels strong emotional responses and is generally responsible for fear and anger—is *less* active following mindfulness meditation practice.[1]

> Though still in its infancy, scientific research on the effects of mindfulness is showing a lot of promise. And, in addition to the ways mindfulness can help students improve, the unsung perk is that mindfulness can easily be introduced by anyone who works with kids, regardless of his or her background.

Similarly, research published in *The Journal of Alternative and Complementary Medicine* suggested that the prefrontal cortex—commonly associated with regulating emotions and behaviors and making wise decisions—is stimulated during periods of quiet meditation.[2] Perhaps most intriguing, a study published in the American Psychological Association's journal, *Emotion*, indicates that the hippocampus—critical to memory and emotional regulation—is *more* active following breath-focused mindfulness training.[3]

Purely from a physiological standpoint, much can be gained by adding a mindfulness practice to *anyone's* daily routine: an uptick in memory, emotional regulation, and decision-making skills just to start. From there, we can project how these gains would be a boon to any classroom.

Benefits in the Classroom

Other studies on the effects of mindfulness show how the techniques can yield valuable results in a classroom setting. For example, one study examined a two-week mindfulness-training course and the effects it had on mind wandering and cognitive performance. The results suggested that mindfulness training improved both reading-comprehension scores and working memory capacity while also reducing the number of distracting thoughts. The researchers concluded that the use of mindfulness techniques is "an effective and efficient technique for improving cognitive function."[4]

David S. Black, director of the BioMind Lab at Keck Medicine of USC, led a field intervention trial at a public elementary school with primarily lower-income and minority children. This study evaluated what effects a five-week mindfulness-based curriculum had on teacher-ratings of student classroom behavior. Results showed that teachers reported improved classroom behavior of their students (for instance, paying attention, self-control, participation in activities, and caring/respect for others) that lasted up to seven weeks post-intervention.[5]

William Kuyken, from the Department of Psychiatry at the University of Oxford, concluded that establishing and maintaining a regular mindfulness practice can lead to less stress while taking tests, which in turn can lead to better scores.[6]

Though still in its infancy, scientific research on the effects of mindfulness is showing a lot of promise. And, in addition to the ways mindfulness can help students improve, the unsung perk is that mindfulness can easily be introduced by anyone who works with kids, regardless of his or her background.

How to Use This Book

My goal with *Mindful Classrooms* was to create an easy-to-use resource that's immediately accessible to all educators. Whatever your role—classroom teacher, resource specialist, paraprofessional, counselor, or any other type of educator—you will be able to inject the activities into the day without taking time away from your established curriculum. Use them at the start of the day, after lunch or recess, during transitions between subjects or activities, or at another time that fits well in your day.

The key benefits to these exercises include: better ability to manage strong emotions, increased empathy for others, heightened focus and memory retention, and better concentration.

The activities in this book consist of five different facets of mindfulness:

- Stretching

- Breathing

- Listening

- Seeing

- Eating

THE LANGUAGE OF MINDFULNESS

The most common mindfulness exercises involve meditation and yoga. However, I won't be using those terms in this book. Instead, I will talk about breathing and stretching. It's much easier to get kids to practice mindfulness using already familiar terms. Additionally, some view meditation and yoga as religious practices, but classroom mindfulness is secular and is not connected with any religion.

These mindfulness activities are broken up into thirty-six weeks to encompass most full school years. Use the activities in order or as best fits your classroom, setting, or group. Each week's entry begins with a suggested weekly schedule of five mindful exercises for each day of the week. Each exercise takes no more than five minutes to complete.

You may choose to do as many of the daily exercises as you like. The best results come from doing at least one stretching and one breathing exercise a day. It can be fairly simple to start each day with three to five minutes of these exercises. Any time of day works but try to make that time consistent to help you and your students benefit the most from daily mindfulness.

Here's an overview of what each activity involves. You'll find specific prompts in each week's activities.

Mindful Stretching

Stretching is a great way to kick off each day. The activities give a new stretch for Monday through Thursday, with review on Friday. Perform each stretch slowly. When you're just starting out, guide students into the pose by using the given scripts. Each pose is accompanied by three slow, deep breaths. You can modify the poses for students who have mobility concerns (see page 174 for suggestions).

Mindful Breathing

Traditionally, mindful breathing is done through the nose (feel free to adjust this for students who find this difficult). Students should use normal in-and-out breaths, not deep breaths. (Unless, of course, a particular script or activity calls for it.) Try mindful breathing after stretching at the start of each day. At first, guide students through five deep breaths ("slowly breathe in, slowly breathe out"). As students improve, set a timer starting at thirty seconds and slowly work your way up to a minute.

While breathing exercises are typically done with eyes closed, be aware some students may not be comfortable doing this. Don't press them on the issue. Invite them to keep their eyes open but to focus on a single spot, rather than looking around.

It's beneficial to have a timer handy when doing mindfulness exercises. You want one you can set for any amount of time up to five minutes (but not one that audibly ticks away the seconds; the noise can be distracting). My favorite is the Insight Timer app. It allows you to set any time increment, choose ambient sounds, and use a number of soothing bell tones to begin or end a breathing session.

Scripts have been provided for different types of breathing. In *guided breathing*, you'll lead students through a breathing exercise, giving them verbal prompts that guide them to think about a social-emotional learning topic. This can lead to silent reflection on the topic or class conversation.

In *intentional breathing*, you lead students through basic breathing exercises to focus on their breath with intent. This helps kids (and adults) feel centered and can help during difficult times that might be caused by strong emotions. This type can also be done during transitions.

Mindful Listening

Encourage students to listen for ambient sounds and either notice the qualities of what they hear or figure out what the sounds are as they transition from one activity to the next. This book emphasizes listening specifically for sounds of nature, nonliving objects, and humans in addition to general listening. Feel free to listen for other categories and/or to randomize the days when specific listening focuses are suggested. This activity is great for transitions between subjects or activities or before moving from one room to another. Mindful listening can also be used as a prompt for journaling, arts integration, self-reflection, and so on. Scripts for mindful listening are on pages 162–165.

Mindful Seeing

Mindful seeing is also a great activity for transition. Encourage students to look around and notice their surroundings in depth and detail. Mindful seeing requires giving thought to every observation. This book emphasizes looking specifically for colors, shapes, and sizes of objects in addition to general seeing. Feel free to look for other categories and/or to randomize the days when specific sight focuses are suggested. Mindful seeing also can be used as a prompt for journaling, arts integration, self-reflection, and so on. Scripts for mindful seeing are on pages 166–169.

MINDFULNESS FOR DE-ESCALATING

Mindful listening and seeing are great strategies for helping escalated students calm down.

- Calmly ask students to start listening mindfully and to name the different sounds they hear. This can help bring students into the present moment and away from the space in their minds that might be causing the escalation.

- Ask students to focus their eyes on something in their surroundings and to describe it in detail. You might prompt them: "What color is it?" "What shapes do you see?"

Mindful Eating

Mindful eating can be used during snack or lunchtime. Mindful eating involves taking one bite at a time and focusing on one sense for a period of time. For example, if students are given slices of oranges during snack time, instruct them to take a moment to look at an orange slice and make silent observations. What do they notice? Then tell them to slowly take one bite. Ask them to chew slowly and swallow that bite. Now, ask them to look at the orange again and notice any changes after that first bite. This activity is best done in silence, so students can focus on their food and then share their experiences with the bite(s). It's a great way to start snack or lunchtime.

When mealtime begins with mindful eating, it becomes a calmer, slower, and more appreciative experience. When things are getting crazy in the cafeteria, try calling for a "mindful eating break" by ringing a chime and leading the cafeteria in one bite at a time for a few bites. It's a great way to help students refocus in a nonpunitive way. Carrcroft Elementary in Wilmington, Delaware, created a mindful eating bulletin board for their cafeteria using student art and phrases (for example, "One Bite at a Time," "Slow Down, Focus on the Taste," and so on) to help remind students about mindfulness in the cafeteria.

If providing treats for the class, please consider any limitations (allergies, religious exemptions, and so on) students may have. It's not important that everyone eats the same thing. What matters is that students observe the experience of eating slowly.

Lunchtime can be a much-needed break for teachers, and they often eat separately from students. In this case, teachers can provide the prompts to students when they drop off students for lunch and then follow up afterward to see how the activity went. Scripts for mindful eating are on pages 170–172.

PREPARING TO EAT MINDFULLY

For the first few weeks, bring some small snacks to class—raisins, marshmallows, and so on—being sure to provide only snacks that accommodate allergies, dietary needs, and religious observances. (Nuts are generally not a good idea.)

It's best to bring food that naturally comes in a small form, so you don't have to break it down. Raisins are great, because students can focus on a single raisin at a time. (It's up to you if you want to pass out more raisins after the exercise is over.)

You can change up this food item each week or, once students become used to how this works, maybe try this exercise during lunch.

Getting Started

One of the best things about these mindfulness exercises is that they don't require any sort of special equipment or preparation. Most stretches can be done within the space it takes to stand or while seated. You'll want to make sure each student has enough space to fully lie down without touching anyone else for some of the more expansive exercises. Kids can do mindful listening, eating, seeing, and breathing from their seats. As noted earlier, you may want to have a timer handy (preferably a silent one, since ticking can be a distraction).

The scripts for mindful seeing, listening, and eating exercises are all located at the back of this book (see pages 160–172) and as downloadable reproducible handouts (see page 181 for information on how to download). Have copies of these scripts ready to go before the start of each exercise. Make notes on your printed scripts of any adaptations you would like to make to fit the specific topic of the week.

Throughout the book, you may notice that some students in the photos are using mats or are barefoot. These are both optional. What's important is that the students are comfortable. If you don't have carpeting, you can still do these practices on the floor or maybe take the students outside.

Before you begin mindful breathing exercises, remind students:

- Whether they're focusing solely on their breath or concentrating on a specific topic, it's okay if their minds wander. This is normal.

- If they find their minds have wandered, they can steer themselves back by taking a slow, deep breath, letting it go, and bringing their thoughts back to the task at hand.

- A wandering mind *does not* mean they've failed. In fact, when they recognize that their thoughts have wandered, they've succeeded in being mindful.

- If students are discouraged because they couldn't stay focused, assure them that the more they do these breathing exercises, the easier it will become to gently recognize their wandering mind and come back to the breath or task at hand. It only takes practice!

Occasionally you may need to modify some of the exercises to accommodate students with varying abilities or change things up to add variety. Suggestions for modifying some of the existing exercises can be found on pages 173–174.

As you begin any mindfulness exercise, ask all students to face one direction. For example, have them all face the front of the room toward you as you lead the practice. If the class is sitting in a circle, have them turn their bodies so they're all facing out once they've received instructions for the practice. This reduces the temptation of looking at their friends and trying to make them laugh. It also can promote self-reflection.

A great way to engage students is to have them take turns leading the mindfulness activities for the class. After you've established a pattern and students understand the exercises, ask for volunteers to take over for a day. It's empowering and promotes peer-to-peer learning. Don't force anyone to lead if he or she is not comfortable, but make sure everyone is given an opportunity.

Lastly, I hope you'll take advantage of this time for yourself by participating in these mindfulness activities with your students. Students can learn faster if new skills are modeled for them. It will be important for you to demonstrate the techniques to help them with their practice. Beyond that, keep in mind that the benefits of mindfulness are available to *everyone*. By establishing your own daily practice, you can boost your personal well-being, ground yourself throughout the course of the day, and find it easier to work with your students. You may even find yourself practicing mindfulness outside the classroom.

> A great way to engage students is to have them take turns leading the mindfulness activities for the class. After you've established a pattern and students understand the exercises, ask for volunteers to take over for a day.

Every technique in this book can be adapted to a solo mindfulness practice. It's not necessary to spend thirty minutes sitting in silent darkness while focusing on your breath. Just a few minutes a day can make a tremendous impact on how we handle ourselves in the classroom. Mindfulness can be practiced:

- first thing after you wake up

- while you're waiting for coffee to brew

- instead of checking your phone for the hundredth time
- while moving from one place to another
- as you lie down for bed at night

The best reason to establish your own mindfulness practice is that students are more likely to "buy in" if they see you performing the exercises too. It might never have occurred to some kids that *your* brain can race a million miles a minute like theirs do or that you can get distracted too. Discussing this with students can be an important part of generating mutual compassion and understanding.

I hope you find these activities easy and fun to do with your students. I would love to hear about your successes with introducing mindfulness into your classroom. Please feel free to reach out to me at:

James Butler
c/o Free Spirit Publishing
6325 Sandburg Road, Suite 100
Minneapolis, MN 55427
james@mindfulclassrooms.com

Best of luck!
James Butler

MINDFULNESS ACTIVITIES
Week by Week

WEEK 1
A-B-C-D Poses & Name Your Feelings

Start the first week of mindfulness exercises slowly. In addition to students who may never have done anything like this before, you'll want to refresh the memories of experienced students.

Be sure your instructions are clear. Find a way to model every exercise.

The following schedule is a suggestion for how to proceed. Feel free to mix things up or to select certain exercises as time allows.

Mindful Breathing

Suggested Week 1 Schedule

	MONDAY	TUESDAY	WEDNESDAY	THURSDAY	FRIDAY
Mindful Stretching	Astronaut	Butterfly	Cat	Downward Dog	REVIEW
Mindful Breathing	Guided Breathing	Intentional Breathing	Guided Breathing	Intentional Breathing	Guided Breathing
Mindful Listening	Listen	Nature	Nonliving Objects	Humans	Listen
Mindful Seeing	See	Colors	Shapes	Sizes	See
Mindful Eating	Smell	Touch	Sight	Hear	Taste

MINDFUL STRETCHING—A-B-C-D POSES ◇ ◇ ◇

ASTRONAUT

1. Stand with your feet together
2. Extend your arms to the side
3. Lift one leg and extend to the side
4. Take three deep breaths
5. Repeat with opposite side

BUTTERFLY

1. Sit straight and tall with the soles of your feet together close to your body
2. Hands on your knees
3. Inhale slowly and lift up your knees
4. Exhale slowly and lower your knees
5. Repeat three times

CAT

1. Start on your hands and knees
2. Arch your back and look between your legs
3. Take three deep breaths

DOWNWARD DOG

1. Start on your hands and knees
2. Straighten your arms and legs while pushing your bottom toward the sky
3. Look between your legs
4. Take three deep breaths

MINDFUL BREATHING ◇ ◇ ◇ ◇ ◇ ◇ ◇ ◇ ◇

GUIDED BREATHING SEL TOPIC
Name Your Feelings (Monday/Wednesday/Friday)

" It's important to name your feelings to help yourself and others understand how you are doing. What feelings did you have on the first day of school?

After a brief discussion about the feelings everyone has named, continue with: **Sit cross-legged on the floor (or comfortably in your chair) with your hands on your knees. Relax your shoulders and close your eyes or look down. Inhale slowly through your nose and exhale slowly through your nose. Let's take five deep breaths together and think about how we felt on the first day of school.**

Inhale . . . exhale . . . (Repeat four more times.)

Slowly open your eyes or look up. Who would like to share how they felt about coming to school today?

If students are slow to discuss their thoughts, get things started by sharing your own feelings. Continue the discussion as time allows.

◇ ◇ ◇ ◇ ◇ ◇ ◇ ◇ ◇ ◇ ◇ ◇ ◇

INTENTIONAL BREATHING
Nose Breathing (Tuesday/Thursday)

" **Today, we are going to do nose breathing. Close your eyes or look down. Relax your body and put your hands on your knees.**

Slowly inhale through your nose and hold for three seconds. One . . . two . . . three . . . Slowly exhale through your nose.

Inhale and hold for three seconds. One . . . two . . . three . . . Exhale slowly. (Repeat inhale-exhale three times.)

◆ MINDFUL LISTENING

This week's mindful listening exercises focus on ambient sounds, sounds of nature, and sounds from nonliving objects. These exercises can be done while seated, standing, or walking from one place to another. If using them during transition, try asking the questions at a stopping point along the way or when you reach your destination.

You'll find mindful listening scripts for each day this week on page 162.

◆ MINDFUL SEEING

This week's mindful seeing exercises focus on noticing the immediate surroundings, noticing colors, and noticing shapes. Like mindful listening, these exercises can be done while seated, standing, or walking from one place to another. If using them during transition, try asking the questions at a stopping point along the way or when you reach your destination.

You'll find mindful seeing scripts for each day this week on page 166.

◆ MINDFUL EATING

This week's mindful eating exercises focus on sense of smell, sense of touch, and sense of sight. These exercises can be done during lunch or snack time. If you supply treats, be sure they come in a naturally small, individual form (raisins are a good example).

You'll find mindful eating scripts for each day this week on page 170.

Fridays are a great day for review. Refresh everyone's memory on how to do the astronaut, butterfly, cat, and downward dog stretching poses. Discuss what it feels like to do each pose. When doing the other exercises, encourage students to make new observations. (For example, ask if students have thought more about how they felt on the first day of school. Have students been aware of naming other feelings during the week?)

WEEK 2
E-F-G-H Poses & Mutual Respect

Mindful Stretching

Suggested Week 2 Schedule

	MONDAY	TUESDAY	WEDNESDAY	THURSDAY	FRIDAY
Mindful Stretching	Elephant	Frog	Gate	Hero	REVIEW
Mindful Breathing	Guided Breathing	Intentional Breathing	Guided Breathing	Intentional Breathing	Guided Breathing
Mindful Listening	Listen	Nature	Nonliving Objects	Humans	Listen
Mindful Seeing	See	Colors	Shapes	Sizes	See
Mindful Eating	Smell	Touch	Sight	Hear	Taste

MINDFUL STRETCHING—E-F-G-H POSES ◇ ◇ ◇

ELEPHANT

1. Stand with feet shoulder-width apart
2. Bend at your waist, look down, and grasp your hands together
3. Inhale slowly and sway to one side
4. Exhale slowly and sway to the other side
5. Repeat three times

FROG

1. Stand with feet shoulder-width apart
2. Looking forward, squat down close to the ground
3. Put your hands on the ground between your legs
4. Take three deep breaths

GATE

1. Start on your knees
2. Extend one leg out to the side
3. Place a hand on your outstretched leg, raise your opposite arm and lean
4. Take three deep breaths
5. Repeat on opposite side

HERO

1. Start on your knees
2. Sit back on your feet
3. Rest your hands on your knees
4. Keep your back straight and look forward
5. Take three deep breaths

MINDFUL BREATHING

GUIDED BREATHING SEL TOPIC
Mutual Respect (Monday/Wednesday/Friday)

Mutual respect means treating other people how you would like to be treated. Why do you think mutual respect is important? When can you show mutual respect?

After a brief discussion about mutual respect, continue with:

Sit cross-legged on the floor (or comfortably in your chair) with your hands on your knees. Relax your shoulders and close your eyes or look down. Breathe in through your nose and out through your nose. Let's practice that. Inhale slowly through your nose and exhale slowly through your nose. Let's take seven deep breaths together and think about how we can show mutual respect.

Inhale . . . exhale . . . (Repeat six more times.)

Slowly open your eyes or look up. Who would like to share how they can show mutual respect?

If students are slow to discuss their thoughts, get things started by sharing your own feelings. Continue the discussion as time allows.

INTENTIONAL BREATHING
Nose-Mouth Breathing (Tuesday/Thursday)

Today, we are going to do nose-mouth breathing. Close your eyes or look down. Relax your body and put your hands on your knees.

Slowly inhale through your *nose* and hold for three seconds. Slowly exhale through your *mouth*.

Inhale and hold for three seconds. Exhale slowly.
(Repeat inhale-exhale six times.)

◆ MINDFUL LISTENING

This week's mindful listening exercises focus on human sounds, nonliving sounds, and sounds from nearby surroundings. These exercises can be done while seated, standing, or walking from one place to another. If using them during transition, try asking the questions at a stopping point along the way or when you reach your destination.

You'll find mindful listening scripts for each day this week on page 162.

◆ MINDFUL SEEING

This week's mindful seeing exercises focus on noticing sizes of objects, noticing colors, and noticing the immediate surroundings. Like mindful listening, these exercises can be done while seated, standing, or walking from one place to another. If using them during transition, try asking the questions at a stopping point along the way or when you reach your destination.

You'll find mindful seeing scripts for each day this week on page 166.

◆ MINDFUL EATING

This week's mindful eating exercises focus on sense of hearing, sense of taste, and sense of touch. These exercises can be done during lunch or snack time. If you supply treats, be sure they come in a naturally small, individual form.

You'll find mindful eating scripts for each day this week on page 170.

Review the week's mindfulness experiences on Friday. Refresh everyone's memory on how to do the elephant, frog, gate, and hero stretching poses. Discuss what it feels like to do each pose. When doing the other exercises, encourage students to make new observations. (For example, ask students if and how they feel differently when breathing through the nose or the mouth.)

WEEK 3
I-J-K-L Poses & Including Others

Mindful Listening

Suggested Week 3 Schedule

	MONDAY	TUESDAY	WEDNESDAY	THURSDAY	FRIDAY
Mindful Stretching	Igloo	Jaguar	Kite	Locust	REVIEW
Mindful Breathing	Guided Breathing	Intentional Breathing	Guided Breathing	Intentional Breathing	Guided Breathing
Mindful Listening	Listen	Nature	Nonliving Objects	Humans	Listen
Mindful Seeing	See	Colors	Shapes	Sizes	See
Mindful Eating	Smell	Touch	Sight	Hear	Taste

MINDFUL STRETCHING—I-J-K-L POSES ◇ ◇ ◇

IGLOO

1. Start on your knees
2. Sit back on your heels and gently bring your forehead to the ground
3. Rest your arms alongside your legs
4. Take three deep breaths

JAGUAR

1. Lie facedown
2. Push your whole body off the ground so you're on your hands and your toes are flexed
3. Lift one leg and extend behind you
4. Take three deep breaths
5. Repeat on the opposite side

KITE

1. Stand with feet together
2. Extend arms above your head and place palms together
3. Inhale slowly and stretch your body to one side
4. Exhale to the middle
5. Repeat three times for each side

LOCUST

1. Lie on your chest
2. Extend your arms in front of you
3. Lift your arms and legs
4. Take three deep breaths

MINDFUL BREATHING

GUIDED BREATHING SEL TOPIC
Including Others (Monday/Wednesday/Friday)

Including others is a form of showing compassion. Have you ever felt left out? How did that feel? What can you do next time you see someone being excluded?

After a brief discussion about including others, continue with:
Sit cross-legged on the floor (or comfortably in your chair) with your hands on your knees. Relax your shoulders and close your eyes or look down. Breathe in through your nose and out through your nose. Let's practice that. Inhale slowly through your nose and exhale slowly through your nose. Let's take ten deep breaths together and think about what we can do if someone is being excluded.

Inhale . . . exhale . . . (Repeat nine more times.)

Slowly open your eyes or look up. Who would like to share what they can do if someone is being excluded?

If students are slow to discuss their thoughts, get things started by sharing your own feelings. Continue the discussion as time allows.

INTENTIONAL BREATHING
Focus on the Breath (Tuesday/Thursday)

Today, we are going to focus on the breath. Close your eyes or look down. Relax your body and put your hands on your knees.

Slowly inhale and focus on breath filling your lungs. Slowly exhale and focus on breath leaving your body.

Inhale slowly and focus on breath. Exhale slowly and focus on breath. (Repeat inhale-exhale eight times.)

◆ MINDFUL LISTENING

This week's mindful listening exercises focus on sounds of nature, sounds from nonliving objects, and ambient sounds. These exercises can be done while seated, standing, or walking from one place to another. If using them during transition, try asking the questions at a stopping point along the way or when you reach your destination.

　　You'll find mindful listening scripts for each day this week on page 162.

◆ MINDFUL SEEING

This week's mindful seeing exercises focus on noticing colors, shapes, and the immediate surroundings. Like mindful listening, these exercises can be done while seated, standing, or walking from one place to another. If using them during transition, try asking the questions at a stopping point along the way or when you reach your destination.

　　You'll find mindful seeing scripts for each day this week on page 166.

◆ MINDFUL EATING

This week's mindful eating exercises focus on sense of sight, sense of smell, and sense of touch. These exercises can be done during lunch or snack time. If you supply treats, be sure they come in a naturally small, individual form.

　　You'll find mindful eating scripts for each day this week on page 170.

On Friday, take a few moments for review. Refresh everyone's memory on how to do the igloo, jaguar, kite, and locust stretching poses. Discuss what it feels like to do each pose. When doing the other exercises, encourage students to make new observations. (For example, ask students what images have stayed with them from their time spent noticing colors and shapes around them.)

WEEK 4
M-N-O-P Poses & Active Listening

Mindful Seeing

Suggested Week 4 Schedule

	MONDAY	TUESDAY	WEDNESDAY	THURSDAY	FRIDAY
Mindful Stretching	Mountain	Ninja	Ostrich	Plank	REVIEW
Mindful Breathing	Guided Breathing	Intentional Breathing	Guided Breathing	Intentional Breathing	Guided Breathing
Mindful Listening	Listen	Nature	Nonliving Objects	Humans	Listen
Mindful Seeing	See	Colors	Shapes	Sizes	See
Mindful Eating	Smell	Touch	Sight	Hear	Taste

MINDFUL STRETCHING—M-N-O-P POSES ◇ ◇ ◇

MOUNTAIN

1. Stand with your feet together
2. Place your palms together in front of your chest
3. Take three deep breaths

NINJA

1. Start in a squatting position
2. Extend one leg out to the side
3. Place elbow on your bent knee and one hand on the ground between legs
4. Take three deep breaths
5. Repeat on opposite side

OSTRICH

1. Stand with your feet together
2. Bend at your waist and hang your arms down toward the ground
3. Look down at the ground
4. Take three deep breaths

PLANK

1. Lie on your chest
2. Place your hands near your shoulders
3. Push your body off the ground so you're on your hands and your toes are flexed
4. Keep your body in a diagonal line
5. Take three deep breaths

MINDFUL BREATHING ◇ ◇ ◇ ◇ ◇ ◇ ◇ ◇ ◇

GUIDED BREATHING SEL TOPIC
Active Listening (Monday/Wednesday/Friday)

Active listening is listening with your ears, eyes, mouth, heart, and whole body. What does it mean to listen with your eyes, and so on? When can you actively listen?

After a brief discussion about active listening, continue with:

Sit cross-legged on the floor (or comfortably in your chair) with your hands on your knees. Relax your shoulders and close your eyes or look down. Slowly breathe in and out through your nose. Let's take ten deep breaths together and think about when we can actively listen.

Inhale . . . exhale . . . (Repeat nine times.)

Slowly open your eyes or look up. Who would like to share when they can actively listen?

If students are slow to discuss their thoughts, get things started by sharing your own feelings. Continue the discussion as time allows.

INTENTIONAL BREATHING
"I Am Strong" (Tuesday/Thursday)

Today, we are going to say "I am strong" in our minds as we breathe. Close your eyes or look down. Relax your body and put your hands on your knees.

Slowly inhale and silently say "I am." Slowly exhale and silently say "strong."

Inhale "I am." Exhale "strong." (Repeat "I Am Strong" breathing eight times.)

◆ MINDFUL LISTENING

This week's mindful listening exercises focus on human sounds, nonliving sounds, and sounds from nearby surroundings. These exercises can be done while seated, standing, or walking from one place to another. If using them during transition, try asking the questions at a stopping point along the way or when you reach your destination.

You'll find mindful listening scripts for each day this week on page 162.

◆ MINDFUL SEEING

This week's mindful seeing exercises focus on noticing the sizes of objects, noticing colors, and noticing the immediate surroundings. Like mindful listening, these exercises can be done while seated, standing, or walking from one place to another. If using them during transition, try asking the questions at a stopping point along the way or when you reach your destination.

You'll find mindful seeing scripts for each day this week on page 166.

◆ MINDFUL EATING

This week's mindful eating exercises focus on sense of hearing, sense of taste, and sense of touch. These exercises can be done during lunch or snack time. If you supply treats, be sure they come in a naturally small, individual form.

You'll find mindful eating scripts for each day this week on page 170.

As you review the week's mindfulness exercises on Friday, refresh everyone's memory on how to do the mountain, ninja, ostrich, and plank stretching poses. What new feelings do students notice as they do the poses again? When doing the other exercises, encourage students to make new observations. (For example, ask students about any new sounds they observed.)

WEEK 5
Q-R-S-T Poses & Ways to Play Fair

Mindful Eating

Suggested Week 5 Schedule

	MONDAY	TUESDAY	WEDNESDAY	THURSDAY	FRIDAY
Mindful Stretching	Queen Dancer	Roadrunner	Snake	Tree	REVIEW
Mindful Breathing	Guided Breathing	Intentional Breathing	Guided Breathing	Intentional Breathing	Guided Breathing
Mindful Listening	Listen	Nature	Nonliving Objects	Humans	Listen
Mindful Seeing	See	Colors	Shapes	Sizes	See
Mindful Eating	Smell	Touch	Sight	Hear	Taste

MINDFUL STRETCHING—Q-R-S-T POSES ◇ ◇ ◇

QUEEN DANCER

1. Stand with your feet together
2. Lift one leg behind you and grab your foot
3. Lift your opposite arm toward the sky
4. Slightly lean forward and take three deep breaths
5. Repeat with opposite side

ROADRUNNER

1. Stand with your feet together
2. Take a big step forward, bend your front knee, and keep your back leg straight
3. Put your hands on the ground on either side of your forward foot
4. Take three deep breaths
5. Repeat with opposite side

SNAKE

1. Lie on your chest
2. Place your hands on the ground on each side of your head
3. Bring your elbows in close to your body
4. Lift up your chest
5. Take three deep breaths

TREE

1. Stand on one leg
2. Place your foot on your standing leg (thigh or calf)
3. Raise your arms above your head and place palms together
4. Take three deep breaths
5. Repeat with opposite side

MINDFUL BREATHING ◇ ◇ ◇ ◇ ◇ ◇ ◇ ◇

GUIDED BREATHING SEL TOPIC
Ways to Play Fair (Monday/Wednesday/Friday)

❝ Three ways to play fair are: play together, trade, or take turns. Can you think of any other ways to play fair? What is a situation that would require playing fair?

After a brief discussion about playing fair, continue with:
Sit cross-legged on the floor (or comfortably in your chair) with your hands on your knees. Relax your shoulders and close your eyes or look down. Breathe in and out through your nose. Now let's breathe together and think about a situation that would require playing fair and how we can play fairly.

Inhale . . . exhale . . . inhale . . . exhale . . . Continue to breathe slowly on your own. (Teacher chooses breathing length, for example, ten breaths, one minute, and so on.)

Slowly open your eyes or look up. Who would like to share how they can play fairly?

If students are slow to discuss their thoughts, get things started by sharing your own feelings. Continue the discussion as time allows.

◇ ◇ ◇ ◇ ◇ ◇ ◇ ◇ ◇ ◇ ◇ ◇ ◇ ◇

INTENTIONAL BREATHING
"I Am Kind" (Tuesday/Thursday)

❝ Today, we are going to say "I am kind" in our minds as we breathe. Close your eyes or look down. Relax your body and put your hands on your knees.

Slowly inhale and silently say "I am." Slowly exhale and silently say "kind."

Inhale "I am." Exhale "kind." (Repeat "I Am Kind" breathing at teacher's discretion, for example, eight times, one minute, and so on.)

◆ MINDFUL LISTENING

This week's mindful listening exercises focus on ambient sounds, sounds of nature, and sounds from nonliving objects. These exercises can be done while seated, standing, or walking from one place to another. If using them during transition, try asking the questions at a stopping point along the way or when you reach your destination.

You'll find mindful listening scripts for each day this week on page 162.

◆ MINDFUL SEEING

This week's mindful seeing exercises focus on noticing the immediate surroundings, noticing colors, and noticing shapes. Like mindful listening, these exercises can be done while seated, standing, or walking from one place to another. If using them during transition, try asking the questions at a stopping point along the way or when you reach your destination.

You'll find mindful seeing scripts for each day this week on page 166.

◆ MINDFUL EATING

This week's mindful eating exercises focus on sense of smell, sense of touch, and sense of sight. These exercises can be done during lunch or snack time. If you supply treats, be sure they come in a naturally small, individual form.

You'll find mindful eating scripts for each day this week on page 170.

Friday review sessions are a chance to make all new mindful observations about the week's exercises. Refresh everyone's memory on how to do the queen dancer, roadrunner, snake, and tree stretching poses. What new feelings do students notice as they do the poses again? When doing the other exercises, encourage students to make new observations. (For example, ask students how their observations of nature may have changed from how they view it every day.)

WEEK 6
U-V-W-X Poses & Compassion

Mindful Breathing

Suggested Week 6 Schedule

	MONDAY	TUESDAY	WEDNESDAY	THURSDAY	FRIDAY
Mindful Stretching	Upward Dog	Volcano	Waterfall	Exhale	REVIEW
Mindful Breathing	Guided Breathing	Intentional Breathing	Guided Breathing	Intentional Breathing	Guided Breathing
Mindful Listening	Listen	Nature	Nonliving Objects	Humans	Listen
Mindful Seeing	See	Colors	Shapes	Sizes	See
Mindful Eating	Smell	Touch	Sight	Hear	Taste

MINDFUL STRETCHING—U-V-W-X POSES ◇ ◇ ◇

UPWARD DOG

1. Lie on your chest
2. Put your hands on the ground by your shoulders
3. Push your upper body off the ground and extend your arms
4. Take three deep breaths

VOLCANO

1. Stand with your feet together
2. Bring your palms together in front of your chest
3. Inhale slowly and push up your hands
4. Exhale slowly and extend your arms to the side
5. Repeat three times

WATERFALL

1. Stand with your feet slightly apart
2. Reach up with your hands
3. Look up
4. Lean back slightly
5. Take three deep breaths

EXHALE

1. Sit cross-legged
2. Put your hands on your knees
3. Close your eyes
4. Take three deep breaths

MINDFUL BREATHING ◇ ◇ ◇ ◇ ◇ ◇ ◇ ◇

GUIDED BREATHING SEL TOPIC
Compassion (Monday/Wednesday/Friday)

Compassion is kindness, caring, and willingness to help others. When have you felt compassion? What is a situation where you could show compassion?

After a brief discussion about compassion, continue with:

Sit cross-legged on the floor (or comfortably in your chair) with your hands on your knees. Relax your shoulders and close your eyes or look down. Breathe in and out through your nose. Now let's breathe together and think about a situation where we could show compassion.

Inhale . . . exhale . . . inhale . . . exhale . . . Continue to breathe slowly on your own. (Teacher chooses breathing length, for example, ten breaths, one minute, and so on.)

Slowly open your eyes or look up. Who would like to share how they can show compassion?

If students are slow to discuss their thoughts, get things started by sharing your own feelings. Continue the discussion as time allows.

INTENTIONAL BREATHING
"I Love Myself" (Tuesday/Thursday)

Today, we are going to say "I love myself" in our minds as we breathe. Close your eyes or look down. Relax your body and put your hands on your knees.

Slowly inhale and silently say "I love." Slowly exhale and silently say "myself."

Inhale "I love."

Exhale "myself." (Repeat "I Love Myself" breathing at teacher's discretion, for example, eight times, one minute, and so on.)

◆ MINDFUL LISTENING

This week's mindful listening exercises focus on sounds of nature, sounds from nonliving objects, and ambient sounds. These exercises can be done while seated, standing, or walking from one place to another. If using them during transition, try asking the questions at a stopping point along the way or when you reach your destination.

You'll find mindful listening scripts for each day this week on page 162.

◆ MINDFUL SEEING

This week's mindful seeing exercises focus on noticing shapes, sizes of objects, and colors. Like mindful listening, these exercises can be done while seated, standing, or walking from one place to another. If using them during transition, try asking the questions at a stopping point along the way or when you reach your destination.

You'll find mindful seeing scripts for each day this week on page 166.

◆ MINDFUL EATING

This week's mindful eating exercises focus on sense of touch, sense of sight, and sense of hearing. These exercises can be done during lunch or snack time. If you supply treats, be sure they come in a naturally small, individual form.

You'll find mindful eating scripts for each day this week on page 170.

Review on Friday gives you and your students a chance to reflect on all you've achieved through mindfulness this week. Refresh everyone's memory on how to do the upward dog, volcano, waterfall, and exhale stretching poses. What new feelings do students notice as they do the poses again? When doing the other exercises, encourage students to make new observations. (For example, ask students for their thoughts on compassion and to brainstorm ideas on how to make the school a more compassionate place.)

WEEK 7
Y-Z & Classic Poses & Courage

Mindful stretching

Suggested Week 7 Schedule

	MONDAY	TUESDAY	WEDNESDAY	THURSDAY	FRIDAY
Mindful Stretching	Yawn	Zebra	Airplane	Child's Pose	REVIEW
Mindful Breathing	Guided Breathing	Intentional Breathing	Guided Breathing	Intentional Breathing	Guided Breathing
Mindful Listening	Listen	Nature	Nonliving Objects	Humans	Listen
Mindful Seeing	See	Colors	Shapes	Sizes	See
Mindful Eating	Smell	Touch	Sight	Hear	Taste

MINDFUL STRETCHING—Y-Z & CLASSIC POSES

YAWN

1. Stand with feet together
2. Extend arms upward diagonally
3. Inhale slowly
4. Exhale with a big yawn and stretch
5. Repeat three times

ZEBRA

1. Stand with feet together and take one big step forward
2. Bend over forward leg and place hands on ankle or shin
3. Take three deep breaths
4. Repeat with opposite side

AIRPLANE

1. Lie on your chest
2. Extend arms out to the side
3. Lift your straightened legs off the ground
4. Lift your chest and look forward
5. Take three deep breaths

CHILD'S POSE

1. Start on your knees
2. Sit back on your heels and gently bring your forehead to the ground
3. Extend your arms in front of you
4. Take three deep breaths

MINDFUL BREATHING ◇ ◇ ◇ ◇ ◇ ◇ ◇ ◇

GUIDED BREATHING SEL TOPIC
Courage (Monday/Wednesday/Friday)

Courage is the strength and ability to do something that frightens you. When have you felt courageous? What is a situation in which you could show courage?

After a brief discussion about courage, continue with:

Sit cross-legged on the floor (or comfortably in your chair) with your hands on your knees. Relax your shoulders and close your eyes or look down. Breathe in and out through your nose. Now let's breathe together and think about a situation where we could show courage.

Inhale . . . exhale . . . inhale . . . exhale . . . Continue to breathe slowly on your own. (Teacher chooses breathing length, for example, ten breaths, one minute, and so on.)

Slowly open your eyes or look up. Who would like to share how they can show courage?

If students are slow to discuss their thoughts, get things started by sharing your own feelings. Continue the discussion as time allows.

◇ ◇ ◇ ◇ ◇ ◇ ◇ ◇ ◇ ◇ ◇ ◇ ◇ ◇ ◇

INTENTIONAL BREATHING
Nose Breathing (Tuesday/Thursday)

Today, we are going to do nose breathing. Close your eyes or look down. Relax your body and put your hands on your knees.

Slowly inhale through your *nose* and hold for three seconds. Slowly exhale through your *nose*.

Inhale and hold for three seconds.

Exhale slowly. (Repeat nose breathing at teacher's discretion, for example, eight times, one minute, and so on.)

◆ MINDFUL LISTENING

This week's mindful listening exercises focus on ambient sounds, sounds of nature, and sounds from nonliving objects. These exercises can be done while seated, standing, or walking from one place to another. If using them during transition, try asking the questions at a stopping point along the way or when you reach your destination.

You'll find mindful listening scripts for each day this week on page 162.

◆ MINDFUL SEEING

This week's mindful seeing exercises focus on noticing the immediate surroundings, noticing colors, and noticing shapes. Like mindful listening, these exercises can be done while seated, standing, or walking from one place to another. If using them during transition, try asking the questions at a stopping point along the way or when you reach your destination.

You'll find mindful seeing scripts for each day this week on page 166.

◆ MINDFUL EATING

This week's mindful eating exercises focus on sense of smell, sense of touch, and sense of sight. These exercises can be done during lunch or snack time. If you supply treats, be sure they come in a naturally small, individual form.

You'll find mindful eating scripts for each day this week on page 170.

This Friday's review marks the start of a new range of stretching poses, moving from A to Z poses to classical poses. Refresh everyone's memory on how to do the yawn, zebra, airplane, and child's pose. What new feelings do students notice as they do the poses again? When doing the other exercises, encourage students to make new observations. (For example, extend the discussion of this week's SEL topic—courage—and ask students to identify examples of courage in their family and friends.)

WEEK 8
School Poses & Self-Talk

Mindful Listening

Suggested Week 8 Schedule

	MONDAY	TUESDAY	WEDNESDAY	THURSDAY	FRIDAY
Mindful Stretching	Pencil	Desk	Book	Sticker	REVIEW
Mindful Breathing	Guided Breathing	Intentional Breathing	Guided Breathing	Intentional Breathing	Guided Breathing
Mindful Listening	Listen	Nature	Nonliving Objects	Humans	Listen
Mindful Seeing	See	Colors	Shapes	Sizes	See
Mindful Eating	Smell	Touch	Sight	Hear	Taste

MINDFUL STRETCHING—SCHOOL POSES ◊ ◊ ◊

PENCIL

1. Stand with your feet together
2. Extend your arms above your head
3. Interlace fingers
4. Take three deep breaths

DESK

1. Start on your hands and knees
2. Place hands directly below shoulders
3. Straighten your back
4. Look down between your hands
5. Take three deep breaths

BOOK

1. Stand with your feet together
2. Squat down while looking forward
3. Bring your arms together in front of you with bent elbows and palms facing you
4. Take three deep breaths

STICKER

1. Lie on your chest
2. Rest your forehead on the ground
3. Extend your arms in front of you on the ground
4. Take three deep breaths

MINDFUL BREATHING ◇ ◇ ◇ ◇ ◇ ◇ ◇ ◇

GUIDED BREATHING SEL TOPIC
Self-Talk (Monday/Wednesday/Friday)

Self-talk is positively talking to yourself about decision-making or self-perception. Examples: "I am strong." "I am smart." "Should I do this?" When could you use self-talk?

After a brief discussion about self-talk, continue with:

Sit cross-legged on the floor (or comfortably in your chair) with your hands on your knees. Relax your shoulders and close your eyes or look down. Breathe in and out through your nose. Now let's breathe together and think about a situation where we could use self-talk.

Inhale . . . exhale . . . inhale . . . exhale . . . Continue to breathe slowly on your own. (Teacher chooses breathing length, for example, ten breaths, one minute, and so on.)

Slowly open your eyes or look up. Who would like to share how they can use self-talk?

If students are slow to discuss their thoughts, get things started by sharing your own feelings. Continue the discussion as time allows.

◇ ◇ ◇ ◇ ◇ ◇ ◇ ◇ ◇ ◇ ◇ ◇ ◇

INTENTIONAL BREATHING
"I Am Strong" (Tuesday/Thursday)

Today, we are going to say "I am strong" in our minds as we breathe. Close your eyes or look down. Relax your body and put your hands on your knees.

Slowly inhale and silently say "I am." Slowly exhale and silently say "strong."

Inhale "I am." Exhale "strong." (Repeat "I Am Strong" breathing at teacher's discretion, for example, eight times, one minute, and so on.)

◆ MINDFUL LISTENING

This week's mindful listening exercises focus on human sounds, nonliving sounds, and sounds from nearby surroundings. These exercises can be done while seated, standing, or walking from one place to another. If using them during transition, try asking the questions at a stopping point along the way or when you reach your destination.

You'll find mindful listening scripts for each day this week on page 162.

◆ MINDFUL SEEING

This week's mindful seeing exercises focus on noticing sizes of objects, noticing colors, and noticing the immediate surroundings. Like mindful listening, these exercises can be done while seated, standing, or walking from one place to another. If using them during transition, try asking the questions at a stopping point along the way or when you reach your destination.

You'll find mindful seeing scripts for each day this week on page 166.

◆ MINDFUL EATING

This week's mindful eating exercises focus on sense of hearing, sense of taste, and sense of touch. These exercises can be done during lunch or snack time. If you supply treats, be sure they come in a naturally small, individual form.

You'll find mindful eating scripts for each day this week on page 170.

A Friday review session can help students retain what they've learned during the week and prompt them to make all new observations. Refresh everyone's memory on how to do the pencil, desk, book, and sticker stretching poses. What new feelings do students notice as they do the poses again? When doing the other exercises, encourage students to make new observations. (For example, extend the discussion of self-talk and ask students to suggest their own positive self-talk for themselves and others.)

WEEK 9
Student Choice & Speak Up

Mindful Seeing

Suggested Week 9 Schedule

	MONDAY	TUESDAY	WEDNESDAY	THURSDAY	FRIDAY
Mindful Stretching	STUDENT CHOICE	STUDENT CHOICE	STUDENT CHOICE	STUDENT CHOICE	REVIEW
Mindful Breathing	Guided Breathing	Intentional Breathing	Guided Breathing	Intentional Breathing	Guided Breathing
Mindful Listening	Listen	Nature	Nonliving Objects	Humans	Listen
Mindful Seeing	See	Colors	Shapes	Sizes	See
Mindful Eating	Smell	Touch	Sight	Hear	Taste

MINDFUL STRETCHING—STUDENT CHOICE ◇   ◇   ◇   ◇   ◇   ◇

Allow students to choose poses from the previous eight weeks or to create their own poses. Ask students who create new poses to teach their poses to the class.

MINDFUL BREATHING ◆ ◆ ◆ ◆ ◆ ◆ ◆ ◆

GUIDED BREATHING SEL TOPIC
Speak Up (Monday/Wednesday/Friday)

" **It's important to speak up when you or someone else is being treated unfairly. Have you ever spoken up for yourself or someone else? When could you speak up?**

After a brief discussion about speaking up, continue with:
Sit cross-legged on the floor (or comfortably in your chair) with your hands on your knees. Relax your shoulders and close your eyes or look down. Breathe in and out through your nose. Now let's breathe together and think about a situation where we could speak up.

Inhale . . . exhale . . . inhale . . . exhale . . . Continue to breathe slowly on your own. (Teacher chooses breathing length, for example, ten breaths, one minute, and so on.)

Slowly open your eyes or look up. Who would like to share how they can speak up?

If students are slow to discuss their thoughts, get things started by sharing your own feelings. Continue the discussion as time allows.

◆ ◆ ◆ ◆ ◆ ◆ ◆ ◆ ◆ ◆ ◆ ◆ ◆ ◆ ◆

INTENTIONAL BREATHING
Nose-Mouth Breathing (Tuesday/Thursday)

" **Today, we are going to do nose-mouth breathing. Close your eyes or look down. Relax your body and put your hands on your knees.**

Slowly inhale through your *nose* and hold for three seconds. Slowly exhale through your *mouth*.

Inhale and hold for three seconds.

Exhale slowly. (Repeat inhale-exhale at teacher's discretion, for example, eight times, one minute, and so on.)

◆ MINDFUL LISTENING

This week's mindful listening exercises focus on ambient sounds, sounds of nature, and sounds from nonliving objects. These exercises can be done while seated, standing, or walking from one place to another. If using them during transition, try asking the questions at a stopping point along the way or when you reach your destination.

You'll find mindful listening scripts for each day this week on page 162.

◆ MINDFUL SEEING

This week's mindful seeing exercises focus on noticing the immediate surroundings, noticing colors, and noticing shapes. Like mindful listening, these exercises can be done while seated, standing, or walking from one place to another. If using them during transition, try asking the questions at a stopping point along the way or when you reach your destination.

You'll find mindful seeing scripts for each day this week on page 166.

◆ MINDFUL EATING

This week's mindful eating exercises focus on sense of smell, sense of touch, and sense of sight. These exercises can be done during lunch or snack time. If you supply treats, be sure they come in a naturally small, individual form.

You'll find mindful eating scripts for each day this week on page 170.

It's week 9, and we're reviewing everything we've learned up to now. Refresh students' memory of all the poses they've done since week 1. As a group, chose any five poses to review. What new feelings do students notice as they do the poses again? When doing the other exercises, encourage students to make new observations. (For example, review the various SEL topics discussed in the last nine weeks and ask students if and how their thoughts have changed on these lessons in that time.)

WEEK 10
Autumn Poses & Honesty

Mindful Eating

Suggested Week 10 Schedule

	MONDAY	TUESDAY	WEDNESDAY	THURSDAY	FRIDAY
Mindful Stretching	Crescent Moon	Bear	Bird	Tractor	REVIEW
Mindful Breathing	Guided Breathing	Intentional Breathing	Guided Breathing	Intentional Breathing	Guided Breathing
Mindful Listening	Listen	Nature	Nonliving Objects	Humans	Listen
Mindful Seeing	See	Colors	Shapes	Sizes	See
Mindful Eating	Smell	Touch	Sight	Hear	Taste

MINDFUL STRETCHING—AUTUMN POSES ◇　◇　◇

CRESCENT MOON

1. Stand with your feet together
2. Extend your arms above your head
3. Place your palms together and lean to one side
4. Take three deep breaths
5. Repeat with opposite side

BEAR

1. Start on your hands and knees
2. Straighten your arms and legs while pushing your bottom up
3. Spread your legs wider than shoulder-width
4. Take three deep breaths

BIRD

1. Stand on one leg
2. Place ankle of lifted leg above knee of standing leg
3. Extend your arms to the side
4. Take three deep breaths
5. Repeat with opposite side

TRACTOR

1. Stand with your feet together
2. Bend your knees and squat down while looking forward
3. Extend your arms in front of you
4. Pretend to grab a steering wheel
5. Take three deep breaths

MINDFUL BREATHING ◇ ◇ ◇ ◇ ◇ ◇ ◇ ◇ ◇

GUIDED BREATHING SEL TOPIC
Honesty (Monday/Wednesday/Friday)

Honesty is being truthful no matter what. Honest people gain the trust of those around them. What is a situation where you've had to be honest? How can you be honest?

After a brief discussion about honesty, continue with:

Sit cross-legged on the floor (or comfortably in your chair) with your hands on your knees. Relax your shoulders and close your eyes or look down. Breathe in and out through your nose. Now let's breathe together and think about a situation where we can be honest.

Inhale . . . exhale . . . inhale . . . exhale . . . Continue to breathe slowly on your own. (Teacher chooses breathing length, for example, ten breaths, one minute, and so on.)

Slowly open your eyes or look up. Who would like to share how they can be honest?

If students are slow to discuss their thoughts, get things started by sharing your own feelings. Continue the discussion as time allows.

◇ ◇ ◇ ◇ ◇ ◇ ◇ ◇ ◇ ◇ ◇ ◇ ◇ ◇ ◇

INTENTIONAL BREATHING
"I Am Kind" (Tuesday/Thursday)

Today, we are going to say "I am kind" in our minds as we breathe. Close your eyes or look down. Relax your body and put your hands on your knees.

Slowly inhale and silently say "I am." Slowly exhale and silently say "kind."

Inhale "I am." Exhale "kind." (Repeat "I Am Kind" breathing at teacher's discretion, for example, eight times, one minute, and so on.)

◆ MINDFUL LISTENING

This week's mindful listening exercises focus on human sounds, nonliving sounds, and sounds from nearby surroundings. These exercises can be done while seated, standing, or walking from one place to another. If using them during transition, try asking the questions at a stopping point along the way or when you reach your destination.

You'll find mindful listening scripts for each day this week on page 162.

◆ MINDFUL SEEING

This week's mindful seeing exercises focus on noticing the sizes of objects, noticing colors, and noticing the immediate surroundings. Like mindful listening, these exercises can be done while seated, standing, or walking from one place to another. If using them during transition, try asking the questions at a stopping point along the way or when you reach your destination.

You'll find mindful seeing scripts for each day this week on page 166.

◆ MINDFUL EATING

This week's mindful eating exercises focus on sense of hearing, sense of taste, and sense of touch. These exercises can be done during lunch or snack time. If you supply treats, be sure they come in a naturally small, individual form.

You'll find mindful eating scripts for each day this week on page 170.

As students' thoughts turn to fall, Friday reviews are a great chance to make mindful observations of the changing seasons. Refresh everyone's memory on how to do the crescent moon, bear, bird, and tractor stretching poses. What new feelings do students notice as they do the poses again? When doing the other exercises, encourage students to make new observations. (For example, ask students to identify any mindful thoughts pertaining specifically to autumn.)

WEEK 11
Tree Life Cycle Poses & Being a Good Friend

Mindful Breathing

Suggested Week 11 Schedule

	MONDAY	TUESDAY	WEDNESDAY	THURSDAY	FRIDAY
Mindful Stretching	Seed	Stem	Leaves	Tree	REVIEW
Mindful Breathing	Guided Breathing	Intentional Breathing	Guided Breathing	Intentional Breathing	Guided Breathing
Mindful Listening	Listen	Nature	Nonliving Objects	Humans	Listen
Mindful Seeing	See	Colors	Shapes	Sizes	See
Mindful Eating	Smell	Touch	Sight	Hear	Taste

MINDFUL STRETCHING—TREE LIFE CYCLE POSES

SEED

1. Start on your knees
2. Sit back on your heels and gently bring your forehead to the ground
3. Wrap your arms around your head
4. Take three deep breaths

STEM

1. Stand with your feet together
2. Hands at your side
3. Close your eyes
4. Take three deep breaths

LEAVES

1. Stand with your feet together
2. Raise your arms diagonally
3. Keeping fingers together, point them down
4. Take three deep breaths

TREE

1. Stand on one leg
2. Place your foot on your standing leg (thigh or calf)
3. Raise your arms above your head and place palms together
4. Take three deep breaths
5. Repeat with opposite side

MINDFUL BREATHING

GUIDED BREATHING SEL TOPIC
Being a Good Friend (Monday/Wednesday/Friday)

Having good friends is a key part of life that requires acting with mutual respect. What makes your friends good friends? How can you be a good friend?

After a brief discussion about being a good friend, continue with:
Sit cross-legged on the floor (or comfortably in your chair) with your hands on your knees. Relax your shoulders and close your eyes or look down. Breathe in and out through your nose. Now let's breathe together and think about how you can be a good friend.

Inhale . . . exhale . . . inhale . . . exhale . . . Continue to breathe slowly on your own. (Teacher chooses breathing length, for example, ten breaths, one minute, and so on.)

Slowly open your eyes or look up. Who would like to share how they can be a good friend?

If students are slow to discuss their thoughts, get things started by sharing your own feelings. Continue the discussion as time allows.

INTENTIONAL BREATHING
Focus on the Breath (Tuesday/Thursday)

Today, we are going to focus on the breath. Close your eyes or look down. Relax your body and put your hands on your knees.

Slowly inhale and focus on breath filling your lungs. Slowly exhale and focus on breath leaving your body.

Inhale slowly and focus on breath. Exhale slowly and focus on breath. (Repeat at teacher's discretion, for example, eight times, one minute, and so on.)

◆ MINDFUL LISTENING

This week's mindful listening exercises focus on sounds of nature, sounds from nonliving objects, and ambient sounds. These exercises can be done while seated, standing, or walking from one place to another. If using them during transition, try asking the questions at a stopping point along the way or when you reach your destination.

You'll find mindful listening scripts for each day this week on page 162.

◆ MINDFUL SEEING

This week's mindful seeing exercises focus on noticing shapes, sizes of objects, and colors. Like mindful listening, these exercises can be done while seated, standing, or walking from one place to another. If using them during transition, try asking the questions at a stopping point along the way or when you reach your destination.

You'll find mindful seeing scripts for each day this week on page 166.

◆ MINDFUL EATING

This week's mindful eating exercises focus on sense of touch, sense of sight, and sense of hearing. These exercises can be done during lunch or snack time. If you supply treats, be sure they come in a naturally small, individual form.

You'll find mindful eating scripts for each day this week on page 170.

Review on Fridays is more than just repeating the week's activities; it represents a chance to see the world through fresh eyes. Refresh everyone's memory on how to do the seed, stem, leaves, and tree stretching poses. What new feelings do students notice as they do the poses again? When doing the other exercises, encourage students to make new observations. (For example, extend the discussion of being a good friend and ask students to create a plan together on how to be a good friend to others.)

WEEK 12
Shape Poses & Integrity

Mindful Stretching

Suggested Week 12 Schedule

	MONDAY	TUESDAY	WEDNESDAY	THURSDAY	FRIDAY
Mindful Stretching	Triangle	Circle	Rectangle	Rhombus	REVIEW
Mindful Breathing	Guided Breathing	Intentional Breathing	Guided Breathing	Intentional Breathing	Guided Breathing
Mindful Listening	Listen	Nature	Nonliving Objects	Humans	Listen
Mindful Seeing	See	Colors	Shapes	Sizes	See
Mindful Eating	Smell	Touch	Sight	Hear	Taste

MINDFUL STRETCHING—SHAPE POSES ◇ ◇ ◇

TRIANGLE

1. Stand with your feet wide apart
2. Bend at your waist and reach down
3. Rest your hands on your shins or ankles
4. Take three deep breaths

CIRCLE

1. Sit cross-legged
2. Reach your arms above your head
3. Round your arms and rest your hands on top of one another
4. Take three deep breaths

RECTANGLE

1. Lie on your chest with your elbows tucked in close to your chest
2. Push up your body onto your elbows and flex your toes
3. Keep your back straight
4. Take three deep breaths

RHOMBUS

1. Stand with your feet together
2. Extend your arms above your head
3. Bend your elbows
4. Touch your fingertips together above your head
5. Take three deep breaths

MINDFUL BREATHING

GUIDED BREATHING SEL TOPIC
Integrity (Monday/Wednesday/Friday)

Integrity is having strong moral principles. It's making good choices even when no one is watching. When have you shown integrity? How can you act with integrity?

After a brief discussion about integrity, continue with:

Sit cross-legged on the floor (or comfortably in your chair) with your hands on your knees. Relax your shoulders and close your eyes or look down. Breathe in and out through your nose. Now let's breathe together and think about a situation where we can act with integrity.

Inhale . . . exhale . . . inhale . . . exhale . . . Continue to breathe slowly on your own. (Teacher chooses breathing length, for example, ten breaths, one minute, and so on.)

Slowly open your eyes or look up. Who would like to share how they can act with integrity?

If students are slow to discuss their thoughts, get things started by sharing your own feelings. Continue the discussion as time allows.

INTENTIONAL BREATHING
"I Love Myself" (Tuesday/Thursday)

Today, we are going to say "I love myself" in our minds as we breathe. Close your eyes or look down. Relax your body and put your hands on your knees.

Slowly inhale and silently say "I love." Slowly exhale and silently say "myself."

Inhale "I love." Exhale "myself." (Repeat "I Love Myself" breathing at teacher's discretion, for example, eight times, one minute, and so on.)

◆ MINDFUL LISTENING

This week's mindful listening exercises focus on ambient sounds, sounds of nature, and sounds from nonliving objects. These exercises can be done while seated, standing, or walking from one place to another. If using them during transition, try asking the questions at a stopping point along the way or when you reach your destination.

You'll find mindful listening scripts for each day this week on page 162.

◆ MINDFUL SEEING

This week's mindful seeing exercises focus on noticing the immediate surroundings, noticing colors, and noticing shapes. Like mindful listening, these exercises can be done while seated, standing, or walking from one place to another. If using them during transition, try asking the questions at a stopping point along the way or when you reach your destination.

You'll find mindful seeing scripts for each day this week on page 166.

◆ MINDFUL EATING

This week's mindful eating exercises focus on sense of smell, sense of touch, and sense of sight. These exercises can be done during lunch or snack time. If you supply treats, be sure they come in a naturally small, individual form.

You'll find mindful eating scripts for each day this week on page 170.

Friday reviews can be a great way to encourage mindfulness when you frame it as seeing something familiar (the past week's exercises) in a new way. Refresh everyone's memory on how to do the triangle, circle, rectangle, and rhombus stretching poses. What new feelings do students notice as they do the poses again? When doing the other exercises, encourage students to make new observations. (For example, ask students to consider any changes they've noticed in themselves since they started the mindfulness exercises.)

WEEK 13
City Poses & Believing in Yourself

Mindful Listening

Suggested Week 13 Schedule

	MONDAY	TUESDAY	WEDNESDAY	THURSDAY	FRIDAY
Mindful Stretching	Bridge	Skyscraper	House	Road	REVIEW
Mindful Breathing	Guided Breathing	Intentional Breathing	Guided Breathing	Intentional Breathing	Guided Breathing
Mindful Listening	Listen	Nature	Nonliving Objects	Humans	Listen
Mindful Seeing	See	Colors	Shapes	Sizes	See
Mindful Eating	Smell	Touch	Sight	Hear	Taste

MINDFUL STRETCHING—CITY POSES ◇ ◇ ◇ ◇

BRIDGE

1. Lie on your chest
2. Place your hands near your shoulders
3. Push your body off the ground so you're on your hands and your toes are flexed
4. Keep your body in a diagonal line
5. Take three deep breaths

SKYSCRAPER

1. Stand with your feet together
2. Lift one knee and raise your opposite arm up toward the sky
3. Take three deep breaths
4. Repeat with opposite side

HOUSE

1. Sit cross-legged
2. Raise your arms above your head
3. Bend your elbows and touch your fingertips together
4. Take three deep breaths

ROAD

1. Lie on your chest
2. Place your arms alongside your body with your palms facing up
3. Rest your chin on the ground
4. Take three deep breaths

MINDFUL BREATHING ◇ ◇ ◇ ◇ ◇ ◇ ◇ ◇

GUIDED BREATHING SEL TOPIC
Believing in Yourself (Monday/Wednesday/Friday)

It's incredibly important to believe in yourself to achieve your goals. When have you believed in yourself? What is a situation where you need to believe in yourself?

After a brief discussion about believing in yourself, continue with:

Sit cross-legged on the floor (or comfortably in your chair) with your hands on your knees. Relax your shoulders and close your eyes or look down. Breathe in and out through your nose. Now let's breathe together and think about a situation where you can believe in yourself.

Inhale . . . exhale . . . inhale . . . exhale . . . Continue to breathe slowly on your own. (Teacher chooses breathing length, for example, ten breaths, one minute, and so on.)

Slowly open your eyes or look up. Who would like to share how they believe in themselves?

If students are slow to discuss their thoughts, get things started by sharing your own feelings. Continue the discussion as time allows.

◇ ◇ ◇ ◇ ◇ ◇ ◇ ◇ ◇ ◇ ◇ ◇ ◇ ◇

INTENTIONAL BREATHING
Nose Breathing (Tuesday/Thursday)

Today, we are going to do nose breathing. Close your eyes or look down. Relax your body and put your hands on your knees.

Slowly inhale through your *nose* and hold for three seconds. Slowly exhale through your *nose*.

Inhale and hold for three seconds. Exhale slowly. (Repeat nose breathing at teacher's discretion, for example, eight times, one minute, and so on.)

◆ MINDFUL LISTENING

This week's mindful listening exercises focus on human sounds, nonliving sounds, and sounds from nearby surroundings. These exercises can be done while seated, standing, or walking from one place to another. If using them during transition, try asking the questions at a stopping point along the way or when you reach your destination.

You'll find mindful listening scripts for each day this week on page 162.

◆ MINDFUL SEEING

This week's mindful seeing exercises focus on noticing sizes of objects, noticing colors, and noticing the immediate surroundings. Like mindful listening, these exercises can be done while seated, standing, or walking from one place to another. If using them during transition, try asking the questions at a stopping point along the way or when you reach your destination.

You'll find mindful seeing scripts for each day this week on page 166.

◆ MINDFUL EATING

This week's mindful eating exercises focus on sense of hearing, sense of taste, and sense of touch. These exercises can be done during lunch or snack time. If you supply treats, be sure they come in a naturally small, individual form.

You'll find mindful eating scripts for each day this week on page 170.

It's good to review the mindfulness exercises on Friday to find new perspectives. Refresh everyone's memory on how to do the bridge, skyscraper, house, and road stretching poses. What new feelings do students notice as they do the poses again? When doing the other exercises, encourage students to make new observations. (For example, extend the discussion of believing in yourself and ask students to name one thing about themselves that they know to be true.)

WEEK 14
Music Poses & Learning from Mistakes

Mindful Seeing

Suggested Week 14 Schedule

	MONDAY	TUESDAY	WEDNESDAY	THURSDAY	FRIDAY
Mindful Stretching	Flute	Drum	Piano	Trumpet	REVIEW
Mindful Breathing	Guided Breathing	Intentional Breathing	Guided Breathing	Intentional Breathing	Guided Breathing
Mindful Listening	Listen	Nature	Nonliving Objects	Humans	Listen
Mindful Seeing	See	Colors	Shapes	Sizes	See
Mindful Eating	Smell	Touch	Sight	Hear	Taste

MINDFUL STRETCHING—MUSIC POSES ◇ ◇ ◇

FLUTE

1. Stand on one leg and rest ankle above knee of standing leg
2. Bring your arms up, bend your elbows and pretend to play a flute
3. Take three deep breaths
4. Repeat with opposite side

DRUM

1. Stand on one leg and rest ankle above knee of standing leg
2. Slowly alternate hands up and down while pretending to play hand drums as you take three deep breaths
3. Repeat with opposite side

PIANO

1. Stand with your feet together
2. Squat down and look forward
3. Raise your arms and pretend to play the piano
4. Slowly move your fingers as you take three deep breaths

TRUMPET

1. Stand on one leg
2. Put two fists together in front of your mouth
3. Slowly inhale and exhale three times pretending to play the trumpet
4. Repeat with opposite side

MINDFUL BREATHING

GUIDED BREATHING SEL TOPICS
Learning from Mistakes (Monday/Wednesday/Friday)

Mistakes happen. They provide opportunities for growth if you learn from them. When have you learned from a mistake? How can you learn from mistakes?

After a brief discussion about learning from mistakes, continue with:

Sit cross-legged on the floor (or comfortably in your chair) with your hands on your knees. Relax your shoulders and close your eyes or look down. Breathe in and out through your nose. Now let's breathe together and think about how we can learn from mistakes.

Inhale . . . exhale . . . inhale . . . exhale . . . Continue to breathe slowly on your own. (Teacher chooses breathing length, for example, ten breaths, one minute, and so on.)

Slowly open your eyes or look up. Who would like to share how they can learn from mistakes?

If students are slow to discuss their thoughts, get things started by sharing your own feelings. Continue the discussion as time allows.

INTENTIONAL BREATHING
"I Am Strong" (Tuesday/Thursday)

Today, we are going to say "I am strong" in our minds as we breathe. Close your eyes or look down. Relax your body and put your hands on your knees.

Slowly inhale and silently say "I am." Slowly exhale and silently say "strong."

Inhale "I am." Exhale "strong." (Repeat "I Am Strong" breathing at teacher's discretion, for example, eight times, one minute, and so on.)

◆ MINDFUL LISTENING

This week's mindful listening exercises focus on sounds of nature, sounds from nonliving objects, and ambient sounds. These exercises can be done while seated, standing, or walking from one place to another. If using them during transition, try asking the questions at a stopping point along the way or when you reach your destination.

You'll find mindful listening scripts for each day this week on page 162.

◆ MINDFUL SEEING

This week's mindful seeing exercises focus on noticing shapes, sizes of objects, and colors. Like mindful listening, these exercises can be done while seated, standing, or walking from one place to another. If using them during transition, try asking the questions at a stopping point along the way or when you reach your destination.

You'll find mindful seeing scripts for each day this week on page 166.

◆ MINDFUL EATING

This week's mindful eating exercises focus on sense of touch, sense of sight, and sense of hearing. These exercises can be done during lunch or snack time. If you supply treats, be sure they come in a naturally small, individual form.

You'll find mindful eating scripts for each day this week on page 170.

End of the week isn't time to take a breather from mindfulness. It's time for reflection. Refresh everyone's memory on how to do the flute, drum, piano, and trumpet stretching poses. What new feelings do students notice as they do the poses again? When doing the other exercises, encourage students to make new observations. (For example, ask students to reflect further on their mindful eating and share what their observations were this week.)

WEEK 15
Light Poses & Gratitude

Mindful Eating

Suggested Week 15 Schedule

	MONDAY	TUESDAY	WEDNESDAY	THURSDAY	FRIDAY
Mindful Stretching	Candle	Lamp	Sun	Moon	REVIEW
Mindful Breathing	Guided Breathing	Intentional Breathing	Guided Breathing	Intentional Breathing	Guided Breathing
Mindful Listening	Listen	Nature	Nonliving Objects	Humans	Listen
Mindful Seeing	See	Colors	Shapes	Sizes	See
Mindful Eating	Smell	Touch	Sight	Hear	Taste

MINDFUL STRETCHING—LIGHT POSES ◇ ◇ ◇

CANDLE

1. Lie on your back
2. Press your arms into the ground
3. Lift your legs straight up
4. Take three deep breaths

LAMP

1. Stand with your feet together
2. Bend your knees and squat down
3. Extend your arms to the side
4. Point your fingers down
5. Take three deep breaths

SUN

1. Stand with your feet together
2. Extend your arms to the side with palms facing up
3. Gently lean back and look up
4. Take three deep breaths

MOON

1. Stand with your feet together
2. Extend your arms above your head
3. Place your palms together and lean to one side
4. Take three deep breaths
5. Repeat with opposite side

MINDFUL BREATHING ◇ ◇ ◇ ◇ ◇ ◇ ◇ ◇

GUIDED BREATHING SEL TOPIC
Gratitude (Monday/Wednesday/Friday)

Gratitude is being thankful and returning kindness given to you. What or who are you thankful for? How can you show gratitude for what you're thankful for?

After a brief discussion about gratitude, continue with:

Sit cross-legged on the floor (or comfortably in your chair) with your hands on your knees. Relax your shoulders and close your eyes or look down. Breathe in and out through your nose. Now let's breathe together and think about what we're thankful for.

Inhale . . . exhale . . . inhale . . . exhale . . . Continue to breathe slowly on your own. (Teacher chooses breathing length, for example, ten breaths, one minute, and so on.)

Slowly open your eyes or look up. Who would like to share what they are thankful for?

If students are slow to discuss their thoughts, get things started by sharing your own feelings. Continue the discussion as time allows.

◇ ◇ ◇ ◇ ◇ ◇ ◇ ◇ ◇ ◇ ◇ ◇ ◇ ◇ ◇

INTENTIONAL BREATHING
Nose-Mouth Breathing (Tuesday/Thursday)

Today, we are going to do nose-mouth breathing. Close your eyes or look down. Relax your body and put your hands on your knees.

Slowly inhale through your *nose* and hold for three seconds. Slowly exhale through your *mouth*.

Inhale and hold for three seconds. Exhale slowly. (Repeat inhale-exhale at teacher's discretion, for example, eight times, one minute, and so on.)

◆ MINDFUL LISTENING

This week's mindful listening exercises focus on ambient sounds, sounds of nature, and sounds from nonliving objects. These exercises can be done while seated, standing, or walking from one place to another. If using them during transition, try asking the questions at a stopping point along the way or when you reach your destination.

You'll find mindful listening scripts for each day this week on page 162.

◆ MINDFUL SEEING

This week's mindful seeing exercises focus on noticing the immediate surroundings, noticing colors, and noticing shapes. Like mindful listening, these exercises can be done while seated, standing, or walking from one place to another. If using them during transition, try asking the questions at a stopping point along the way or when you reach your destination.

You'll find mindful seeing scripts for each day this week on page 166.

◆ MINDFUL EATING

This week's mindful eating exercises focus on sense of smell, sense of touch, and sense of sight. These exercises can be done during lunch or snack time. If you supply treats, be sure they come in a naturally small, individual form.

You'll find mindful eating scripts for each day this week on page 170.

When reviewing your mindfulness exercises on Friday, encourage discussion: What were some favorite exercises? What new thoughts did students have? Refresh everyone's memory on how to do the candle, lamp, sun, and moon stretching poses. What new feelings do students notice as they do the poses again? When doing the other exercises, encourage students to make new observations. (For example, ask students to share their thoughts on the different shapes they considered this week.)

WEEK 16
Animal Poses & Generosity

Mindful Breathing

Suggested Week 16 Schedule

	MONDAY	TUESDAY	WEDNESDAY	THURSDAY	FRIDAY
Mindful Stretching	Lion	Leopard	Elephant	Rhino	REVIEW
Mindful Breathing	Guided Breathing	Intentional Breathing	Guided Breathing	Intentional Breathing	Guided Breathing
Mindful Listening	Listen	Nature	Nonliving Objects	Humans	Listen
Mindful Seeing	See	Colors	Shapes	Sizes	See
Mindful Eating	Smell	Touch	Sight	Hear	Taste

MINDFUL STRETCHING—ANIMAL POSES ◇ ◇ ◇

LION

1. Start on your knees
2. Sit back on your heels
3. Place your hands on your knees
4. Take three deep lion breaths

LEOPARD

1. Start in downward dog
2. Lift one leg straight behind you
3. Take three deep breaths
4. Repeat with opposite side

ELEPHANT

1. Stand with feet shoulder-width apart
2. Bend at your waist, look down, and grasp your hands together
3. Inhale slowly and sway to one side
4. Exhale slowly and sway to the other side
5. Repeat three times

RHINO

1. Start in plank pose
2. Lift one arm straight in front of you
3. Take three deep breaths
4. Repeat with opposite side

MINDFUL BREATHING

GUIDED BREATHING SEL TOPIC
Generosity (Monday/Wednesday/Friday)

Generosity is showing kindness to others through actions, service, or gifts. When have you felt generosity? How can you act with generosity?

After a brief discussion about generosity, continue with:

Sit cross-legged on the floor (or comfortably in your chair) with your hands on your knees. Relax your shoulders and close your eyes or look down. Breathe in and out through your nose. Now let's breathe together and think about a situation where we can act with generosity.

Inhale . . . exhale . . . inhale . . . exhale . . . Continue to breathe slowly on your own. (Teacher chooses breathing length, for example, ten breaths, one minute, and so on.)

Slowly open your eyes or look up. Who would like to share how they can be generous?

If students are slow to discuss their thoughts, get things started by sharing your own feelings. Continue the discussion as time allows.

INTENTIONAL BREATHING
"I Am Kind" (Tuesday/Thursday)

Today, we are going to say "I am kind" in our minds as we breathe. Close your eyes or look down. Relax your body and put your hands on your knees.

Slowly inhale and silently say "I am." Slowly exhale and silently say "kind."

Inhale "I am." Exhale "kind." (Repeat "I Am Kind" breathing at teacher's discretion, for example, eight times, one minute, and so on.)

◆ MINDFUL LISTENING

This week's mindful listening exercises focus on human sounds, nonliving sounds, and sounds from nearby surroundings. These exercises can be done while seated, standing, or walking from one place to another. If using them during transition, try asking the questions at a stopping point along the way or when you reach your destination.

You'll find mindful listening scripts for each day this week on page 162.

◆ MINDFUL SEEING

This week's mindful seeing exercises focus on noticing sizes of objects, noticing colors, and noticing the immediate surroundings. Like mindful listening, these exercises can be done while seated, standing, or walking from one place to another. If using them during transition, try asking the questions at a stopping point along the way or when you reach your destination.

You'll find mindful seeing scripts for each day this week on page 166.

◆ MINDFUL EATING

This week's mindful eating exercises focus on sense of hearing, sense of taste, and sense of touch. These exercises can be done during lunch or snack time. If you supply treats, be sure they come in a naturally small, individual form.

You'll find mindful eating scripts for each day this week on page 170.

Fridays are a great day to review the various mindful thoughts everyone has had all week. Refresh everyone's memory on how to do the lion, leopard, elephant, and rhino stretching poses. What new feelings do students notice as they do the poses again? When doing the other exercises, encourage students to make new observations. (For example, ask students to consider their thoughts on this week's SEL topic: generosity. What does generosity mean to them and how do they see it in their family and friends?)

WEEK 17
Winter Poses & Self-Compassion

Mindful Stretching

Suggested Week 17 Schedule

	MONDAY	TUESDAY	WEDNESDAY	THURSDAY	FRIDAY
Mindful Stretching	Mountain Top	Pine Tree	Ice Skater	Skier	REVIEW
Mindful Breathing	Guided Breathing	Intentional Breathing	Guided Breathing	Intentional Breathing	Guided Breathing
Mindful Listening	Listen	Nature	Nonliving Objects	Humans	Listen
Mindful Seeing	See	Colors	Shapes	Sizes	See
Mindful Eating	Smell	Touch	Sight	Hear	Taste

MINDFUL STRETCHING—WINTER POSES ◇ ◇ ◇

MOUNTAIN TOP

1. Stand with your feet together
2. Extend your arms above your head
3. Place your palms together
4. Take three deep breaths

PINE TREE

1. Stand on one leg
2. Place your foot on your standing leg
3. Raise your arms above your head and place palms together
4. Take three deep breaths
5. Repeat with opposite side

ICE SKATER

1. Stand with your feet together
2. Lift one leg behind you and grab your foot
3. Lift your opposite arm toward the sky
4. Take three deep breaths
5. Repeat with opposite side

SKIER

1. Stand with feet shoulder-width apart and hands at your side
2. Bend your knees and squat down
3. Bend your elbows and bring your hands up pretending to hold ski poles
4. Take three deep breaths

MINDFUL BREATHING

GUIDED BREATHING SEL TOPIC
Self-compassion (Monday/Wednesday/Friday)

Self-compassion is loving yourself and giving yourself kindness. Why do you think self-compassion is important? How can you be self-compassionate?

After a brief discussion about self-compassion, continue with:
Sit cross-legged on the floor (or comfortably in your chair) with your hands on your knees. Relax your shoulders and close your eyes or look down. Breathe in and out through your nose. Now let's breathe together and think about how you can be compassionate toward yourself.

Inhale . . . exhale . . . inhale . . . exhale . . . Continue to breathe slowly on your own. (Teacher chooses breathing length, for example, ten breaths, one minute, and so on.)

Slowly open your eyes or look up. Who would like to share how you can be compassionate toward yourself?

If students are slow to discuss their thoughts, get things started by sharing your own feelings. Continue the discussion as time allows.

◊ ◊ ◊ ◊ ◊ ◊ ◊ ◊ ◊ ◊ ◊ ◊ ◊ ◊

INTENTIONAL BREATHING
Focus on the Breath (Tuesday/Thursday)

Today, we are going to focus on the breath. Close your eyes or look down. Relax your body and put your hands on your knees.

Slowly inhale and focus on breath filling your lungs. Slowly exhale and focus on breath leaving your body.

Inhale slowly and focus on breath. Exhale slowly and focus on breath. (Repeat at teacher's discretion, for example, eight times, one minute, and so on.)

◆ MINDFUL LISTENING

This week's mindful listening exercises focus on sounds of nature, sounds from nonliving objects, and ambient sounds. These exercises can be done while seated, standing, or walking from one place to another. If using them during transition, try asking the questions at a stopping point along the way or when you reach your destination.

You'll find mindful listening scripts for each day this week on page 162.

◆ MINDFUL SEEING

This week's mindful seeing exercises focus on noticing shapes, sizes of objects, and colors. Like mindful listening, these exercises can be done while seated, standing, or walking from one place to another. If using them during transition, try asking the questions at a stopping point along the way or when you reach your destination.

You'll find mindful seeing scripts for each day this week on page 166.

◆ MINDFUL EATING

This week's mindful eating exercises focus on sense of touch, sense of sight, and sense of hearing. These exercises can be done during lunch or snack time. If you supply treats, be sure they come in a naturally small, individual form.

You'll find mindful eating scripts for each day this week on page 170.

A Friday review session can help students retain what they've learned during the week and prompt them to make all new observations. Refresh everyone's memory on how to do the mountain top, pine tree, ice skater, and skier stretching poses. What new feelings do students notice as they do the poses again? When doing the other exercises, encourage students to make new observations. (For example, ask students what they learned this week when they took time to mindfully smell their food. What new thoughts came to mind?)

WEEK 18
Student Choice & Positivity

Mindful Listening

Suggested Week 18 Schedule

	MONDAY	TUESDAY	WEDNESDAY	THURSDAY	FRIDAY
Mindful Stretching	STUDENT CHOICE	STUDENT CHOICE	STUDENT CHOICE	STUDENT CHOICE	REVIEW
Mindful Breathing	Guided Breathing	Intentional Breathing	Guided Breathing	Intentional Breathing	Guided Breathing
Mindful Listening	Listen	Nature	Nonliving Objects	Humans	Listen
Mindful Seeing	See	Colors	Shapes	Sizes	See
Mindful Eating	Smell	Touch	Sight	Hear	Taste

MINDFUL STRETCHING—STUDENT CHOICE

Allow students to choose poses from the previous eight weeks (or any poses since the beginning of the school year) or to create their own poses. Ask students who create new poses to teach their poses to the class.

MINDFUL BREATHING ◇ ◇ ◇ ◇ ◇ ◇ ◇ ◇ ◇

GUIDED BREATHING SEL TOPIC
POSITIVITY (Monday/Wednesday/Friday)

Positivity is focusing on goodness and happiness in your world. Why do you think it's important to be positive? What positive things or people do you have in your life?

After a brief discussion about positivity, continue with:

Sit cross-legged on the floor (or comfortably in your chair) with your hands on your knees. Relax your shoulders and close your eyes or look down. Breathe in and out through your nose. Now let's breathe together and think about something or someone positive in your life.

Inhale . . . exhale . . . inhale . . . exhale . . . Continue to breathe slowly on your own. (Teacher chooses breathing length, for example, ten breaths, one minute, and so on.)

Slowly open your eyes or look up. Who would like to share about something or someone positive?

If students are slow to discuss their thoughts, get things started by sharing your own feelings. Continue the discussion as time allows.

◇ ◇ ◇ ◇ ◇ ◇ ◇ ◇ ◇ ◇ ◇ ◇ ◇ ◇

INTENTIONAL BREATHING
"I Love Myself" (Tuesday/Thursday)

Today, we are going to say "I love myself" in our minds as we breathe. Close your eyes or look down. Relax your body and put your hands on your knees.

Slowly inhale and silently say "I love." Slowly exhale and silently say "myself."

Inhale "I love." Exhale "myself." (Repeat "I Love Myself" breathing at teacher's discretion, for example, eight times, one minute, and so on.)

◆ MINDFUL LISTENING

This week's mindful listening exercises focus on ambient sounds, sounds of nature, and sounds from nonliving objects. These exercises can be done while seated, standing, or walking from one place to another. If using them during transition, try asking the questions at a stopping point along the way or when you reach your destination.

You'll find mindful listening scripts for each day this week on page 162.

◆ MINDFUL SEEING

This week's mindful seeing exercises focus on noticing the immediate surroundings, noticing colors, and noticing shapes. Like mindful listening, these exercises can be done while seated, standing, or walking from one place to another. If using them during transition, try asking the questions at a stopping point along the way or when you reach your destination.

You'll find mindful seeing scripts for each day this week on page 166.

◆ MINDFUL EATING

This week's mindful eating exercises focus on sense of smell, sense of touch, and sense of sight. These exercises can be done during lunch or snack time. If you supply treats, be sure they come in a naturally small, individual form.

You'll find mindful eating scripts for each day this week on page 170.

This is the halfway point! Friday review will look at all the mindfulness exercises the students have studied so far. Remind students of all the stretching poses they've learned in the last nine weeks (or, if you're feeling adventurous, remind them of everything since the beginning). As a group, choose five stretching poses to review. What new feelings do students notice as they do the poses again? When doing the other exercises, encourage students to make new observations. (For example, ask students to reflect on the halfway point of the school year. What does it mean to them? How do they see it differently when they consider everything mindfully?)

WEEK 19
HOPE Poses & Seeking Help

Mindful Seeing

Suggested Week 19 Schedule

	MONDAY	TUESDAY	WEDNESDAY	THURSDAY	FRIDAY
Mindful Stretching	Happy Baby	Otter	Pencil	Eagle	REVIEW
Mindful Breathing	Guided Breathing	Intentional Breathing	Guided Breathing	Intentional Breathing	Guided Breathing
Mindful Listening	Listen	Nature	Nonliving Objects	Humans	Listen
Mindful Seeing	See	Colors	Shapes	Sizes	See
Mindful Eating	Smell	Touch	Sight	Hear	Taste

MINDFUL STRETCHING—HOPE POSES ◇   ◇   ◇

HAPPY BABY

1. Lie on your back
2. Lift up your legs
3. Reach up and grab the outside of your feet
4. Take three deep breaths

OTTER

1. Lie on your chest
2. Put your hands on the ground by your shoulders
3. Push your upper body off the ground and extend your arms
4. Take three deep breaths

PENCIL

1. Stand with your feet together
2. Extend your arms above your head
3. Interlace fingers
4. Take three deep breaths

EAGLE

1. Stand with your feet together and bend your knees
2. Lift one leg and wrap it in front of your standing leg
3. Cross your arms in front of your chest and place your palms together
4. Take three deep breaths
5. Repeat with opposite side

MINDFUL BREATHING ◇ ◇ ◇ ◇ ◇ ◇ ◇ ◇

GUIDED BREATHING SEL TOPIC
Seeking Help (Monday/Wednesday/Friday)

It's okay to seek help to solve a problem (after trying to resolve it on your own or in an emergency). When have you sought help? When is a good time to seek help?

After a brief discussion about seeking help, continue with:

Sit cross-legged on the floor (or comfortably in your chair) with your hands on your knees. Relax your shoulders and close your eyes or look down. Breathe in and out through your nose. Now let's breathe together and think about a time when you might need to seek help.

Inhale . . . exhale . . . inhale . . . exhale . . . Continue to breathe slowly on your own. (Teacher chooses breathing length, for example, ten breaths, one minute, and so on.)

Slowly open your eyes or look up. Who would like to share about when they might need to seek help?

If students are slow to discuss their thoughts, get things started by sharing your own feelings. Continue the discussion as time allows.

◇ ◇ ◇ ◇ ◇ ◇ ◇ ◇ ◇ ◇ ◇ ◇ ◇

INTENTIONAL BREATHING
Nose Breathing (Tuesday/Thursday)

Today, we are going to do nose breathing. Close your eyes or look down. Relax your body and put your hands on your knees.

Slowly inhale through your *nose* and hold the breath for three seconds. Slowly exhale through your *nose*.

Inhale and hold for three seconds. Exhale slowly. (Repeat nose breathing at teacher's discretion, for example, eight times, one minute, and so on.)

◆ MINDFUL LISTENING

This week's mindful listening exercises focus on human sounds, nonliving sounds, and sounds from nearby surroundings. These exercises can be done while seated, standing, or walking from one place to another. If using them during transition, try asking the questions at a stopping point along the way or when you reach your destination.

You'll find mindful listening scripts for each day this week on page 162.

◆ MINDFUL SEEING

This week's mindful seeing exercises focus on noticing sizes of objects, noticing colors, and noticing the immediate surroundings. Like mindful listening, these exercises can be done while seated, standing, or walking from one place to another. If using them during transition, try asking the questions at a stopping point along the way or when you reach your destination.

You'll find mindful seeing scripts for each day this week on page 166.

◆ MINDFUL EATING

This week's mindful eating exercises focus on sense of hearing, sense of taste, and sense of touch. These exercises can be done during lunch or snack time. If you supply treats, be sure they come in a naturally small, individual form.

You'll find mindful eating scripts for each day this week on page 170.

Review the week's mindfulness experiences on Friday. Refresh everyone's memory on how to do the happy baby, otter, pencil, and eagle stretching poses. What new feelings do students notice as they do the poses again? When doing the other exercises, encourage students to make new observations. (For example, extend the discussion of seeking help and create a class list of ways to help others who need it.)

WEEK 20
READ Poses & Perseverance

Mindful Eating

Suggested Week 20 Schedule

	MONDAY	TUESDAY	WEDNESDAY	THURSDAY	FRIDAY
Mindful Stretching	Roadrunner	Exhale	Astronaut	Deuces	REVIEW
Mindful Breathing	Guided Breathing	Intentional Breathing	Guided Breathing	Intentional Breathing	Guided Breathing
Mindful Listening	Listen	Nature	Nonliving Objects	Humans	Listen
Mindful Seeing	See	Colors	Shapes	Sizes	See
Mindful Eating	Smell	Touch	Sight	Hear	Taste

MINDFUL STRETCHING—READ POSES ◇ ◇ ◇

ROADRUNNER

1. Stand with your feet together
2. Take a big step forward, bend your front, knee and keep your back leg straight
3. Put your hands on the ground on either side of your forward foot
4. Take three deep breaths
5. Repeat with opposite side

EXHALE

1. Sit cross-legged
2. Put your hands on your knees
3. Close your eyes
4. Take three deep breaths

ASTRONAUT

1. Stand with your feet together
2. Extend your arms to the side
3. Lift one leg and extend to the side
4. Take three deep breaths
5. Repeat with opposite side

DEUCES

1. Start on one knee
2. Place one hand on the leg kneeling down
3. Rest your elbow on your bent knee and make the "peace sign"
4. Take three deep breaths
5. Repeat with opposite side

MINDFUL BREATHING ◇ ◇ ◇ ◇ ◇ ◇ ◇ ◇

GUIDED BREATHING SEL TOPIC
Perseverance (Monday/Wednesday/Friday)

Perseverance is continued effort to do something despite difficulty or delayed success. When have you persevered? How can you show perseverance?

After a brief discussion about perseverance, continue with:

Sit cross-legged on the floor (or comfortably in your chair) with your hands on your knees. Relax your shoulders and close your eyes or look down. Breathe in and out through your nose. Let's practice that. Inhale slowly through your nose and exhale slowly through your nose. Let's breathe together and think about how we can show perseverance.

Inhale . . . exhale . . . inhale . . . exhale . . . Continue to breathe slowly on your own. (Teacher chooses breathing length, for example, ten breaths, one minute, and so on.)

Slowly open your eyes or look up. Who would like to share how they can show perseverance?

If students are slow to discuss their thoughts, get things started by sharing your own feelings. Continue the discussion as time allows.

◇ ◇ ◇ ◇ ◇ ◇ ◇ ◇ ◇ ◇ ◇ ◇ ◇

INTENTIONAL BREATHING
"I Am Strong" (Tuesday/Thursday)

Today, we are going to say "I am strong" in our minds as we breathe. Close your eyes or look down. Relax your body and put your hands on your knees.

Slowly inhale and silently say "I am." Slowly exhale and silently say "strong."

Inhale "I am." Exhale "strong." (Repeat at teacher's discretion, for example, eight times, one minute, and so on.)

◆ MINDFUL LISTENING

This week's mindful listening exercises focus on sounds of nature, sounds from nonliving objects, and ambient sounds. These exercises can be done while seated, standing, or walking from one place to another. If using them during transition, try asking the questions at a stopping point along the way or when you reach your destination.

You'll find mindful listening scripts for each day this week on page 162.

◆ MINDFUL SEEING

This week's mindful seeing exercises focus on noticing shapes, sizes of objects, and colors. Like mindful listening, these exercises can be done while seated, standing, or walking from one place to another. If using them during transition, try asking the questions at a stopping point along the way or when you reach your destination.

You'll find mindful seeing scripts for each day this week on page 166.

◆ MINDFUL EATING

This week's mindful eating exercises focus on sense of touch, sense of sight, and sense of hearing. These exercises can be done during lunch or snack time. If you supply treats, be sure they come in a naturally small, individual form.

You'll find mindful eating scripts for each day this week on page 170.

On Friday, take a few moments for review. Refresh everyone's memory on how to do the roadrunner, exhale, astronaut, and deuces stretching poses. What new feelings do students notice as they do the poses again? When doing the other exercises, encourage students to make new observations. (For example, ask students for their thoughts on the sounds from nonliving objects they noticed this week.)

WEEK 21
LOVE Poses & Adapting to Change

Mindful Breathing

Suggested Week 21 Schedule

	MONDAY	TUESDAY	WEDNESDAY	THURSDAY	FRIDAY
Mindful Stretching	Locust	Open	Volcano	Elephant	REVIEW
Mindful Breathing	Guided Breathing	Intentional Breathing	Guided Breathing	Intentional Breathing	Guided Breathing
Mindful Listening	Listen	Nature	Nonliving Objects	Humans	Listen
Mindful Seeing	See	Colors	Shapes	Sizes	See
Mindful Eating	Smell	Touch	Sight	Hear	Taste

MINDFUL STRETCHING—LOVE POSES ◆   ◆   ◆   ◆

LOCUST (VARIATION)

1. Lie on your chest
2. Reach your arms behind you and grasp your hands together
3. Lift your chest and your legs off the ground
4. Take three deep breaths

OPEN

1. Lie on your chest
2. Bend your knees and lift up your legs
3. Reach your arms behind you and grab your legs
4. Lift your chest off the ground
5. Take three deep breaths

VOLCANO

1. Stand with your feet together
2. Bring your palms together in front of your chest
3. Inhale slowly and push up your hands
4. Exhale slowly and extend your arms to the side
5. Repeat three times

ELEPHANT

1. Stand with feet shoulder-width apart
2. Bend at your waist, look down, and grasp your hands together
3. Inhale slowly and sway to one side
4. Exhale slowly and sway to the other side
5. Repeat three times

MINDFUL BREATHING

> ### GUIDED BREATHING SEL TOPIC
> ### Adapting to Change (Monday/Wednesday/Friday)
>
> It's important to learn how to adjust to new life/routine conditions. When have you had to adapt to change? What could you do if conditions changed today?

After a brief discussion about adapting to change, continue with:

Sit cross-legged on the floor (or comfortably in your chair) with your hands on your knees. Relax your shoulders and close your eyes or look down. Breathe in and out through your nose. Now let's breathe together and think about what we could do if conditions changed today and we had to adapt.

Inhale . . . exhale . . . inhale . . . exhale . . . Continue to breathe slowly on your own. (Teacher chooses breathing length, for example, ten breaths, one minute, and so on.)

Slowly open your eyes or look up. Who would like to share about what they would do if they had to adapt to change today?

If students are slow to discuss their thoughts, get things started by sharing your own feelings. Continue the discussion as time allows.

> ### INTENTIONAL BREATHING
> ### Nose-Mouth Breathing (Tuesday/Thursday)
>
> **Today, we are going to do nose-mouth breathing. Close your eyes or look down. Relax your body and put your hands on your knees.**

Slowly inhale through your *nose* and hold for three seconds. Slowly exhale through your *mouth*.

Inhale and hold for three seconds. Exhale slowly. (Repeat inhale-exhale at teacher's discretion, for example, eight times, one minute, and so on.)

◆ MINDFUL LISTENING

This week's mindful listening exercises focus on ambient sounds, sounds of nature, and sounds from nonliving objects. These exercises can be done while seated, standing, or walking from one place to another. If using them during transition, try asking the questions at a stopping point along the way or when you reach your destination.

You'll find mindful listening scripts for each day this week on page 162.

◆ MINDFUL SEEING

This week's mindful seeing exercises focus on noticing the immediate surroundings, noticing colors, and noticing shapes. Like mindful listening, these exercises can be done while seated, standing, or walking from one place to another. If using them during transition, try asking the questions at a stopping point along the way or when you reach your destination.

You'll find mindful seeing scripts for each day this week on page 166.

◆ MINDFUL EATING

This week's mindful eating exercises focus on sense of smell, sense of touch, and sense of sight. These exercises can be done during lunch or snack time. If you supply treats, be sure they come in a naturally small, individual form.

You'll find mindful eating scripts for each day this week on page 170.

If possible, try something new this Friday for review. Can you take the class to a new location within the school to do their exercises? Can you go outside? Can you add soft music to stretching time? Refresh everyone's memory on how to do the locust, open, volcano, and elephant stretching poses. What new feelings do students notice as they do the poses again? When doing the other exercises, encourage students to make new observations. (For example, extend the discussion on adapting to change. What was it like to adapt to the change of doing mindfulness exercises every day?)

WEEK 22
Warrior Poses & Empathy

Mindful Stretching

Suggested Week 22 Schedule

	MONDAY	TUESDAY	WEDNESDAY	THURSDAY	FRIDAY
Mindful Stretching	Warrior 1	Warrior 2	Warrior 3	Reverse Warrior	REVIEW
Mindful Breathing	Guided Breathing	Intentional Breathing	Guided Breathing	Intentional Breathing	Guided Breathing
Mindful Listening	Listen	Nature	Nonliving Objects	Humans	Listen
Mindful Seeing	See	Colors	Shapes	Sizes	See
Mindful Eating	Smell	Touch	Sight	Hear	Taste

MINDFUL STRETCHING—WARRIOR POSES ◊ ◊ ◊

WARRIOR I

1. Stand and take one big step forward, bending your front knee
2. Raise your arms above your head
3. Take three deep breaths
4. Repeat with opposite side

WARRIOR 2

1. Stand and take one big step forward, bending your front knee
2. Rotate your back foot and point your chest in same direction
3. Raise your arms over your legs and look past fingertips of hand above bent knee
4. Take three deep breaths
5. Repeat with opposite side

WARRIOR 3

1. Stand on one leg
2. Extend one leg behind you
3. Bend at your waist and extend your arms in front of you
4. Take three deep breaths
5. Repeat with opposite side

REVERSE WARRIOR

1. Stand and take one big step forward, bending your front knee
2. Rotate your back foot and point your chest in same direction
3. Gently lean back resting hand on straight leg and raising opposite arm up and back
4. Take three deep breaths
5. Repeat with opposite side

MINDFUL BREATHING

GUIDED BREATHING SEL TOPIC
Empathy (Monday/Wednesday/Friday)

Empathy is understanding and sharing the feelings of another. When have you felt empathy? How could you show empathy for someone else today?

After a brief discussion about empathy, continue with:

Sit cross-legged on the floor (or comfortably in your chair) with your hands on your knees. Relax your shoulders and close your eyes or look down. Breathe in and out through your nose. Now let's breathe together and think about how we can show empathy for others today.

Inhale . . . exhale . . . inhale . . . exhale . . . Continue to breathe slowly on your own. (Teacher chooses breathing length, for example, ten breaths, one minute, and so on.)

Slowly open your eyes or look up. Who would like to share about how they can show empathy?

If students are slow to discuss their thoughts, get things started by sharing your own feelings. Continue the discussion as time allows.

INTENTIONAL BREATHING
"I Am Kind" (Tuesday/Thursday)

Today, we are going to say "I am kind" in our minds as we breathe. Close your eyes or look down. Relax your body and put your hands on your knees.

Slowly inhale and silently say "I am." Slowly exhale and silently say "kind."

Inhale "I am." Exhale "kind." (Repeat "I Am Kind" breathing at teacher's discretion, for example, eight times, one minute, and so on.)

◆ MINDFUL LISTENING

This week's mindful listening exercises focus on ambient sounds, sounds of nature, and sounds from nonliving objects. These exercises can be done while seated, standing, or walking from one place to another. If using them during transition, try asking the questions at a stopping point along the way or when you reach your destination.

You'll find mindful listening scripts for each day this week on page 162.

◆ MINDFUL SEEING

This week's mindful seeing exercises focus on noticing the immediate surroundings, noticing colors, and noticing shapes. Like mindful listening, these exercises can be done while seated, standing, or walking from one place to another. If using them during transition, try asking the questions at a stopping point along the way or when you reach your destination.

You'll find mindful seeing scripts for each day this week on page 166.

◆ MINDFUL EATING

This week's mindful eating exercises focus on sense of smell, sense of touch, and sense of sight. These exercises can be done during lunch or snack time. If you supply treats, be sure they come in a naturally small, individual form.

You'll find mindful eating scripts for each day this week on page 170.

Friday review is a great way to remind everyone that even though you may have observed something once, there are still other ways to observe when you encounter that something again. Refresh everyone's memory on how to do the warrior 1, warrior 2, warrior 3, and reverse warrior stretching poses. What new feelings do students notice as they do the poses again? When doing the other exercises, encourage students to make new observations. (For example, the theme of this week's stretching poses is warriors. This suggests strength. Discuss how being mindful in all you do can make you strong.)

WEEK 23
Furniture Poses & Saying Problems Without Blame

Mindful Listening

Suggested Week 23 Schedule

	MONDAY	TUESDAY	WEDNESDAY	THURSDAY	FRIDAY
Mindful Stretching	Table	Chair	Couch	Shelf	REVIEW
Mindful Breathing	Guided Breathing	Intentional Breathing	Guided Breathing	Intentional Breathing	Guided Breathing
Mindful Listening	Listen	Nature	Nonliving Objects	Humans	Listen
Mindful Seeing	See	Colors	Shapes	Sizes	See
Mindful Eating	Smell	Touch	Sight	Hear	Taste

MINDFUL STRETCHING—FURNITURE POSES ◇   ◇

TABLE

1. Start on your hands and knees
2. Place hands directly below shoulders
3. Straighten your back
4. Look down between your hands
5. Take three deep breaths

CHAIR

1. Stand with your feet together
2. Look forward
3. Bend your knees and squat down
4. Raise your arms above your head
5. Take three deep breaths

COUCH

1. Lie on your side
2. Rest your top arm on your thigh
3. Bend your bottom arm and rest your head on your hand
4. Take three deep breaths
5. Repeat with opposite side

SHELF

1. Lie on your back
2. Place your arms on the ground beside your body
3. Lift up your legs straight
4. Bend your knees and keep your feet parallel to the ground
5. Take three deep breaths

MINDFUL BREATHING

GUIDED BREATHING SEL TOPIC
Saying Problems Without Blame
(Monday/Wednesday/Friday)

Saying a problem without blaming someone else is a problem-solving skill. For example, avoid saying "You always. . . ." and instead say "It makes me feel [blank] when [blank]." How could you say a problem today without blame?

After a brief discussion about saying problems without blame, continue with: **Sit cross-legged on the floor (or comfortably in your chair) with your hands on your knees. Relax your shoulders and close your eyes or look down. Breathe in and out through your nose. Now let's breathe together and think about how we can say a problem without blame.**

Inhale . . . exhale . . . inhale . . . exhale . . . Continue to breathe slowly on your own. (Teacher chooses breathing length, for example, ten breaths, one minute, and so on.)

Slowly open your eyes or look up. Who would like to share about how they can say a problem without blame?

If students are slow to discuss their thoughts, get things started by sharing your own feelings. Continue the discussion as time allows.

◆   ◆   ◆   ◆   ◆   ◆   ◆   ◆   ◆   ◆   ◆   ◆   ◆   ◆

INTENTIONAL BREATHING
FOCUS on the Breath (Tuesday/Thursday)

Today, we are going to focus on the breath. Close your eyes or look down. Relax your body and put your hands on your knees.

Slowly inhale and focus on breath filling your lungs. Slowly exhale and focus on breath leaving your body.

Inhale slowly and focus on breath. Exhale slowly and focus on breath. (Repeat at teacher's discretion, for example, eight times, one minute, and so on.)

◆ MINDFUL LISTENING

This week's mindful listening exercises focus on human sounds, nonliving sounds, and sounds from nearby surroundings. These exercises can be done while seated, standing, or walking from one place to another. If using them during transition, try asking the questions at a stopping point along the way or when you reach your destination.

You'll find mindful listening scripts for each day this week on page 162.

◆ MINDFUL SEEING

This week's mindful seeing exercises focus on noticing sizes of objects, noticing colors, and noticing the immediate surroundings. Like mindful listening, these exercises can be done while seated, standing, or walking from one place to another. If using them during transition, try asking the questions at a stopping point along the way or when you reach your destination.

You'll find mindful seeing scripts for each day this week on page 166.

◆ MINDFUL EATING

This week's mindful eating exercises focus on sense of hearing, sense of taste, and sense of touch. These exercises can be done during lunch or snack time. If you supply treats, be sure they come in a naturally small, individual form.

You'll find mindful eating scripts for each day this week on page 170.

Make Friday review sessions an oasis at the end of the week. Try adding some restful elements to the environment: Play calming music, turn down the lights, and so on. Refresh everyone's memory on how to do the table, chair, couch, and shelf stretching poses. What new feelings do students notice as they do the poses again? When doing the other exercises, encourage students to make new observations. (For example, ask students to reflect on the mindful seeing exercise and what they noticed in their surroundings. How has that changed from day to day?)

WEEK 24
Flying B Poses & Strong Feelings

Mindful Seeing

Suggested Week 24 Schedule

	MONDAY	TUESDAY	WEDNESDAY	THURSDAY	FRIDAY
Mindful Stretching	Bee	Butterfly	Bird	Bat	REVIEW
Mindful Breathing	Guided Breathing	Intentional Breathing	Guided Breathing	Intentional Breathing	Guided Breathing
Mindful Listening	Listen	Nature	Nonliving Objects	Humans	Listen
Mindful Seeing	See	Colors	Shapes	Sizes	See
Mindful Eating	Smell	Touch	Sight	Hear	Taste

MINDFUL STRETCHING—FLYING B POSES ◇ ◇ ◇

BEE

1. Start on your knees
2. Gently place your forehead on the ground
3. Reach your arms behind you and grasp your hands together
4. Lift your arms toward the sky
5. Take three deep breaths

BUTTERFLY (VARIATION)

1. Sit straight and tall with the soles of your feet together close to your body
2. Bring your palms together in front of your chest
3. Inhale slowly and lift up your knees
4. Exhale slowly and lower your knees
5. Repeat three times

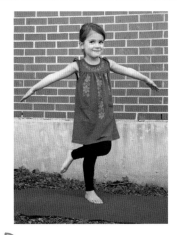

BIRD

1. Stand on one leg
2. Place ankle of lifted leg above knee of standing leg
3. Extend your arms to the side
4. Take three deep breaths
5. Repeat with opposite side

BAT

1. Lie on your back
2. Bend your elbows and place your hands on your shoulders
3. Lift up your legs straight
4. Take three deep breaths

MINDFUL BREATHING ◇ ◇ ◇ ◇ ◇ ◇ ◇ ◇

GUIDED BREATHING SEL TOPIC
Strong Feelings (Monday/Wednesday/Friday)

It's okay to have strong feelings. It's important to manage them appropriately. When have you felt strong feelings? How can you calm down when strong feelings arise?

After a brief discussion about strong feelings, continue with:

Sit cross-legged on the floor (or comfortably in your chair) with your hands on your knees. Relax your shoulders and close your eyes or look down. Breathe in and out through your nose. Now let's breathe together and think about how you can calm down when you have strong feelings.

Inhale . . . exhale . . . inhale . . . exhale . . . Continue to breathe slowly on your own. (Teacher chooses breathing length, for example, ten breaths, one minute, and so on.)

Slowly open your eyes or look up. Who would like to share about how they can calm down when they have strong feelings?

If students are slow to discuss their thoughts, get things started by sharing your own feelings. Continue the discussion as time allows.

◇ ◇ ◇ ◇ ◇ ◇ ◇ ◇ ◇ ◇ ◇ ◇ ◇ ◇

INTENTIONAL BREATHING
"I Love Myself" (Tuesday/Thursday)

Today, we are going to say "I love myself" in our minds as we breathe. Close your eyes or look down. Relax your body and put your hands on your knees.

Slowly inhale and silently say "I love." Slowly exhale and silently say "myself."

Inhale "I love." Exhale "myself." (Repeat "I Love Myself" breathing at teacher's discretion, for example, eight times, one minute, and so on.)

◆ MINDFUL LISTENING

This week's mindful listening exercises focus on sounds of nature, sounds from nonliving objects, and ambient sounds. These exercises can be done while seated, standing, or walking from one place to another. If using them during transition, try asking the questions at a stopping point along the way or when you reach your destination.

You'll find mindful listening scripts for each day this week on page 162.

◆ MINDFUL SEEING

This week's mindful seeing exercises focus on noticing shapes, sizes of objects, and colors. Like mindful listening, these exercises can be done while seated, standing, or walking from one place to another. If using them during transition, try asking the questions at a stopping point along the way or when you reach your destination.

You'll find mindful seeing scripts for each day this week on page 166.

◆ MINDFUL EATING

This week's mindful eating exercises focus on sense of touch, sense of sight, and sense of hearing. These exercises can be done during lunch or snack time. If you supply treats, be sure they come in a naturally small, individual form.

You'll find mindful eating scripts for each day this week on page 170.

As you review this week's mindfulness exercises on Friday, refresh everyone's memory on how to do the bee, butterfly, bird, and bat stretching poses. What new feelings do students notice as they do the poses again? When doing the other exercises, encourage students to make new observations. (For example, extend the discussion of strong feelings and create a class list of ways to calm down when needed.)

WEEK 25
CALM Poses & Courtesy

Mindful Eating

Suggested Week 25 Schedule

	MONDAY	TUESDAY	WEDNESDAY	THURSDAY	FRIDAY
Mindful Stretching	Cow	Airplane	Lion	Mountain	REVIEW
Mindful Breathing	Guided Breathing	Intentional Breathing	Guided Breathing	Intentional Breathing	Guided Breathing
Mindful Listening	Listen	Nature	Nonliving Objects	Humans	Listen
Mindful Seeing	See	Colors	Shapes	Sizes	See
Mindful Eating	Smell	Touch	Sight	Hear	Taste

MINDFUL STRETCHING—CALM POSES ◇ ◇ ◇ ◇

COW

1. Start on your hands and knees
2. Curl your back and look up
3. Take three deep breaths

AIRPLANE

1. Lie on your chest
2. Extend arms out to the side
3. Lift your straightened legs off the ground
4. Lift your chest and look forward
5. Take three deep breaths

LION

1. Start on your knees
2. Sit back on your heels
3. Place your hands on your knees
4. Take three deep lion breaths

MOUNTAIN

1. Stand with your feet together
2. Place your palms together in front of your chest
3. Take three deep breaths

MINDFUL BREATHING ◇ ◇ ◇ ◇ ◇ ◇ ◇ ◇ ◇

GUIDED BREATHING SEL TOPIC
courtesy (Monday/Wednesday/Friday)

Courtesy is being polite to others and showing good manners such as saying "please" and "thank you." When have you been courteous? How can you show courtesy today?

After a brief discussion about courtesy, continue with:

Sit cross-legged on the floor (or comfortably in your chair) with your hands on your knees. Relax your shoulders and close your eyes or look down. Breathe in and out through your nose. Now let's breathe together and think about how we can show courtesy.

Inhale . . . exhale . . . inhale . . . exhale . . . Continue to breathe slowly on your own. (Teacher chooses breathing length, for example, ten breaths, one minute, and so on.)

Slowly open your eyes or look up. Who would like to share about how they can show courtesy?

If students are slow to discuss their thoughts, get things started by sharing your own feelings. Continue the discussion as time allows.

◇ ◇ ◇ ◇ ◇ ◇ ◇ ◇ ◇ ◇ ◇ ◇ ◇ ◇

INTENTIONAL BREATHING
Nose Breathing (Tuesday/Thursday)

Today, we are going to do nose breathing. Close your eyes or look down. Relax your body and put your hands on your knees.

Slowly inhale through your *nose* and hold for three seconds. Slowly exhale through your *nose*.

Inhale and hold for three seconds. Exhale slowly. (Repeat inhale-exhale at teacher's discretion, for example, eight times, one minute, and so on.)

◆ MINDFUL LISTENING

This week's mindful listening exercises focus on human sounds, nonliving sounds, and sounds from nearby surroundings. These exercises can be done while seated, standing, or walking from one place to another. If using them during transition, try asking the questions at a stopping point along the way or when you reach your destination.

You'll find mindful listening scripts for each day this week on page 162.

◆ MINDFUL SEEING

This week's mindful seeing exercises focus on noticing sizes of objects, noticing colors, and noticing the immediate surroundings. Like mindful listening, these exercises can be done while seated, standing, or walking from one place to another. If using them during transition, try asking the questions at a stopping point along the way or when you reach your destination.

You'll find mindful seeing scripts for each day this week on page 166.

◆ MINDFUL EATING

This week's mindful eating exercises focus on sense of hearing, sense of taste, and sense of touch. These exercises can be done during lunch or snack time. If you supply treats, be sure they come in a naturally small, individual form.

You'll find mindful eating scripts for each day this week on page 170.

This Friday as you review the mindfulness exercises, remember to reflect as a group on the progress you've made. Refresh everyone's memory on how to do the cow, airplane, lion, and mountain stretching poses. What new feelings do students notice as they do the poses again? When doing the other exercises, encourage students to make new observations. (For example, ask students if they have performed mindful eating outside of school and what they have noticed.)

WEEK 26
REST Poses & Patience

Mindful Breathing

Suggested Week 26 Schedule

	MONDAY	TUESDAY	WEDNESDAY	THURSDAY	FRIDAY
Mindful Stretching	Roadrunner	Eagle	Sticker	Table	REVIEW
Mindful Breathing	Guided Breathing	Intentional Breathing	Guided Breathing	Intentional Breathing	Guided Breathing
Mindful Listening	Listen	Nature	Nonliving Objects	Humans	Listen
Mindful Seeing	See	Colors	Shapes	Sizes	See
Mindful Eating	Smell	Touch	Sight	Hear	Taste

MINDFUL STRETCHING—REST POSES ◇ ◇ ◇ ◇

ROADRUNNER

1. Stand with your feet together
2. Take a big step forward, bend your front knee, and keep your back leg straight
3. Put your hands on the ground on either side of your forward foot
4. Take three deep breaths
5. Repeat with opposite side

EAGLE

1. Stand with your feet together and bend your knees
2. Lift one leg and wrap it in front of your standing leg
3. Cross your arms in front of your chest and place your palms together
4. Take three deep breaths
5. Repeat with opposite side

STICKER

1. Lie on your chest
2. Rest your forehead on the ground
3. Extend your arms in front of you on the ground
4. Take three deep breaths

TABLE

1. Start on your hands and knees
2. Place hands directly below shoulders
3. Straighten your back
4. Look down between your hands
5. Take three deep breaths

MINDFUL BREATHING

GUIDED BREATHING SEL TOPIC
Patience (Monday/Wednesday/Friday)

Patience is remaining calm during difficult situations. When is a time you have had to show patience? What can you do if you're in a situation that requires patience?

After a brief discussion about patience, continue with:

Sit cross-legged on the floor (or comfortably in your chair) with your hands on your knees. Relax your shoulders and close your eyes or look down. Breathe in and out through your nose. Now let's breathe together and think about what we can do if we're in a situation that requires patience.

Inhale . . . exhale . . . inhale . . . exhale . . . Continue to breathe slowly on your own. (Teacher chooses breathing length, for example, ten breaths, one minute, and so on.)

Slowly open your eyes or look up. Who would like to share about what they can do if they are in a situation that requires patience?

If students are slow to discuss their thoughts, get things started by sharing your own feelings. Continue the discussion as time allows.

INTENTIONAL BREATHING
"I Am Strong" (Tuesday/Thursday)

Today, we are going to say "I am strong" in our minds as we breathe. Close your eyes or look down. Relax your body and put your hands on your knees.

Slowly inhale and silently say "I am." Slowly exhale and silently say "strong."

Inhale "I am." Exhale "strong." (Repeat "I Am Strong" breathing at teacher's discretion, for example, eight times, one minute, and so on.)

◆ MINDFUL LISTENING

This week's mindful listening exercises focus on sounds of nature, sounds from nonliving objects, and ambient sounds. These exercises can be done while seated, standing, or walking from one place to another. If using them during transition, try asking the questions at a stopping point along the way or when you reach your destination.

You'll find mindful listening scripts for each day this week on page 162.

◆ MINDFUL SEEING

This week's mindful seeing exercises focus on noticing shapes, sizes of objects, and colors. Like mindful listening, these exercises can be done while seated, standing, or walking from one place to another. If using them during transition, try asking the questions at a stopping point along the way or when you reach your destination.

You'll find mindful seeing scripts for each day this week on page 166.

◆ MINDFUL EATING

This week's mindful eating exercises focus on sense of touch, sense of sight, and sense of hearing. These exercises can be done during lunch or snack time. If you supply treats, be sure they come in a naturally small, individual form.

You'll find mindful eating scripts for each day this week on page 170.

Encourage the class to reflect on the entire week when you review on Friday. Refresh everyone's memory on how to do the roadrunner, eagle, sticker, and table stretching poses. What new feelings do students notice as they do the poses again? When doing the other exercises, encourage students to make new observations. (For example, ask students to consider the human sounds they've noticed this week and share anything they found surprising.)

WEEK 27
Student Choice & Forgiving Others

Mindful stretching

Suggested Week 27 Schedule

	MONDAY	TUESDAY	WEDNESDAY	THURSDAY	FRIDAY
Mindful Stretching	STUDENT CHOICE	STUDENT CHOICE	STUDENT CHOICE	STUDENT CHOICE	REVIEW
Mindful Breathing	Guided Breathing	Intentional Breathing	Guided Breathing	Intentional Breathing	Guided Breathing
Mindful Listening	Listen	Nature	Nonliving Objects	Humans	Listen
Mindful Seeing	See	Colors	Shapes	Sizes	See
Mindful Eating	Smell	Touch	Sight	Hear	Taste

MINDFUL STRETCHING—STUDENT CHOICE ◇ ◇ ◇ ◇ ◇ ◇

Allow students to choose poses from the previous eight weeks (or any poses since the beginning of the school year) or to create their own poses. Ask students who create new poses to teach their poses to the class.

MINDFUL BREATHING ◇ ◇ ◇ ◇ ◇ ◇ ◇ ◇

GUIDED BREATHING SEL TOPIC
Forgiving Others (Monday/Wednesday/Friday)

Forgiveness is when you let go of negative emotions regarding an incident. When have you forgiven someone? What is a situation where you can show forgiveness?

After a brief discussion about forgiveness, continue with:

Sit cross-legged on the floor (or comfortably in your chair) with your hands on your knees. Relax your shoulders and close your eyes or look down. Breathe in and out through your nose. Now let's breathe together and think about a situation where you can forgive someone.

Inhale . . . exhale . . . inhale . . . exhale . . . Continue to breathe slowly on your own. (Teacher chooses breathing length, for example, ten breaths, one minute, and so on.)

Slowly open your eyes or look up. Who would like to share about a situation where they can forgive someone?

If students are slow to discuss their thoughts, get things started by sharing your own feelings. Continue the discussion as time allows.

◇ ◇ ◇ ◇ ◇ ◇ ◇ ◇ ◇ ◇ ◇ ◇ ◇ ◇

INTENTIONAL BREATHING
Nose-Mouth Breathing (Tuesday/Thursday)

Today, we are going to do nose-mouth breathing. Close your eyes or look down. Relax your body and put your hands on your knees.

Slowly inhale through your *nose* and hold for three seconds. Slowly exhale through your *mouth*.

Inhale and hold for three seconds. Exhale slowly. (Repeat inhale-exhale at teacher's discretion, for example, eight times, one minute, and so on.)

◆ MINDFUL LISTENING

This week's mindful listening exercises focus on ambient sounds, sounds of nature, and sounds from nonliving objects. These exercises can be done while seated, standing, or walking from one place to another. If using them during transition, try asking the questions at a stopping point along the way or when you reach your destination.

You'll find mindful listening scripts for each day this week on page 162.

◆ MINDFUL SEEING

This week's mindful seeing exercises focus on noticing the immediate surroundings, noticing colors, and noticing shapes. Like mindful listening, these exercises can be done while seated, standing, or walking from one place to another. If using them during transition, try asking the questions at a stopping point along the way or when you reach your destination.

You'll find mindful seeing scripts for each day this week on page 166.

◆ MINDFUL EATING

This week's mindful eating exercises focus on sense of smell, sense of touch, and sense of sight. These exercises can be done during lunch or snack time. If you supply treats, be sure they come in a naturally small, individual form.

You'll find mindful eating scripts for each day this week on page 170.

This week means we are three-quarters through the exercises. Time has really flown and everyone has come so far. Be sure to congratulate everyone. Take time to refresh everyone's memory on all the stretching poses learned in the last nine weeks. As a group, choose five poses to review. What new feelings do students notice as they do the poses again? When doing the other exercises, encourage students to make new observations. (For example, extend the discussion of this week's SEL topic—forgiving others—and ask for mindful observations of times when it's been hard to forgive.)

WEEK 28
Sports Poses & Anxiety/Worry

Mindful Listening

Suggested Week 28 Schedule

	MONDAY	TUESDAY	WEDNESDAY	THURSDAY	FRIDAY
Mindful Stretching	Baseball	Basketball	Football	Soccer	REVIEW
Mindful Breathing	Guided Breathing	Intentional Breathing	Guided Breathing	Intentional Breathing	Guided Breathing
Mindful Listening	Listen	Nature	Nonliving Objects	Humans	Listen
Mindful Seeing	See	Colors	Shapes	Sizes	See
Mindful Eating	Smell	Touch	Sight	Hear	Taste

MINDFUL STRETCHING—SPORTS POSES ◇ ◇ ◇

BASEBALL

1. Stand on one leg with your other knee bent and thigh parallel to the ground
2. Place one fist into the palm of your other hand in front of your chest
3. Take three deep breaths
4. Repeat with opposite side

BASKETBALL

1. Stand with your legs far apart
2. Extend your arms to the side
3. Bend your knees and squat down
4. Take three deep breaths

FOOTBALL

1. Stand with one leg raised, knee bent
2. Using the same arm as your standing leg, pretend you're holding a football
3. Extend your opposite arm to the side
4. Take three deep breaths
5. Repeat with opposite side

SOCCER

1. Take one big step forward, shift your weight over your front foot
2. Lift your back leg behind you
3. Extend one arm in front of you and one arm along your back leg
4. Take three deep breaths
5. Repeat with opposite side

MINDFUL BREATHING ◇ ◇ ◇ ◇ ◇ ◇ ◇ ◇

GUIDED BREATHING SEL TOPIC
Anxiety/Worry (Monday/Wednesday/Friday)

Anxiety is feeling worried about something. When have you felt worried about something? How did you deal with it? What can you do to calm down if you feel anxious?

After a brief discussion about anxiety, continue with:

Sit cross-legged on the floor (or comfortably in your chair) with your hands on your knees. Relax your shoulders and close your eyes or look down. Breathe in and out through your nose. Now let's breathe together and think about what we can do if we feel anxious or worried.

Inhale . . . exhale . . . inhale . . . exhale . . . Continue to breathe slowly on your own. (Teacher chooses breathing length, for example, ten breaths, one minute, and so on.)

Slowly open your eyes or look up. Who would like to share about what they can do if they feel anxious or worried?

If students are slow to discuss their thoughts, get things started by sharing your own feelings. Continue the discussion as time allows.

◇ ◇ ◇ ◇ ◇ ◇ ◇ ◇ ◇ ◇ ◇ ◇ ◇ ◇

INTENTIONAL BREATHING
"I Am Kind" (Tuesday/Thursday)

Today, we are going to say "I am kind" in our minds as we breathe. Close your eyes or look down. Relax your body and put your hands on your knees.

Slowly inhale and silently say "I am." Slowly exhale and silently say "kind."

Inhale "I am." Exhale "kind."
(Repeat "I Am Kind" breathing at teacher's discretion, for example, eight times, one minute, and so on.)

◆ MINDFUL LISTENING

This week's mindful listening exercises focus on human sounds, nonliving sounds, and sounds from nearby surroundings. These exercises can be done while seated, standing, or walking from one place to another. If using them during transition, try asking the questions at a stopping point along the way or when you reach your destination.

You'll find mindful listening scripts for each day this week on page 162.

◆ MINDFUL SEEING

This week's mindful seeing exercises focus on noticing sizes of objects, noticing colors, and noticing the immediate surroundings. Like mindful listening, these exercises can be done while seated, standing, or walking from one place to another. If using them during transition, try asking the questions at a stopping point along the way or when you reach your destination.

You'll find mindful seeing scripts for each day this week on page 166.

◆ MINDFUL EATING

This week's mindful eating exercises focus on sense of hearing, sense of taste, and sense of touch. These exercises can be done during lunch or snack time. If you supply treats, be sure they come in a naturally small, individual form.

You'll find mindful eating scripts for each day this week on page 170.

Fridays are all about reflection and remembering to stay in the present moment. Refresh everyone's memory on how to do the baseball, basketball, football, and soccer stretching poses. What new feelings do students notice as they do the poses again? When doing the other exercises, encourage students to make new observations. (For example, ask students to share some of the observations they had all week when they were mindfully seeing.)

WEEK 29
Butterfly Life Cycle Poses
& Respecting Differences

Mindful Seeing

Suggested Week 29 Schedule

	MONDAY	TUESDAY	WEDNESDAY	THURSDAY	FRIDAY
Mindful Stretching	Egg	Caterpillar	Chrysalis	Butterfly	REVIEW
Mindful Breathing	Guided Breathing	Intentional Breathing	Guided Breathing	Intentional Breathing	Guided Breathing
Mindful Listening	Listen	Nature	Nonliving Objects	Humans	Listen
Mindful Seeing	See	Colors	Shapes	Sizes	See
Mindful Eating	Smell	Touch	Sight	Hear	Taste

MINDFUL STRETCHING— BUTTERFLY LIFE CYCLE POSES ◇ ◇ ◇ ◇ ◇ ◇

EGG

1. Start on your knees
2. Sit back on your heels and gently bring your forehead to the ground
3. Wrap your arms around your head
4. Take three deep breaths

CATERPILLAR

1. Lie on your chest with your elbows tucked in close to your chest
2. Push your body up onto your elbows and toes
3. Keep your back straight
4. Take three deep breaths

CHRYSALIS

1. Stand with your feet together
2. Bend at your waist and hang your arms down toward the ground
3. Look down at the ground
4. Take three deep breaths

BUTTERFLY (VARIATION)

1. Sit straight and tall with the soles of your feet together close to your body
2. Hands on your ankles
3. Inhale slowly and lift up your knees
4. Exhale slowly and lower your knees
5. Repeat three times

MINDFUL BREATHING

GUIDED BREATHING SEL TOPIC
Respecting Differences
(Monday/Wednesday/Friday)

Being different is beautiful. Everyone is different in one way or another. How are you different? What can we do to respect people's differences?

After a brief discussion about respecting differences, continue with:

Sit cross-legged on the floor (or comfortably in your chair) with your hands on your knees. Relax your shoulders and close your eyes or look down. Breathe in and out through your nose. Now let's breathe together and think about how we can respect people's differences.

Inhale . . . exhale . . . inhale . . . exhale . . . Continue to breathe slowly on your own. (Teacher chooses breathing length, for example, ten breaths, one minute, and so on.)

Slowly open your eyes or look up. Who would like to share about how they can respect people's differences?

If students are slow to discuss their thoughts, get things started by sharing your own feelings. Continue the discussion as time allows.

INTENTIONAL BREATHING
Focus on the Breath (Tuesday/Thursday)

Today, we are going to focus on the breath. Close your eyes or look down. Relax your body and put your hands on your knees.

Slowly inhale and focus on breath filling your lungs. Slowly exhale and focus on breath leaving your body.

Inhale slowly and focus on breath. Exhale slowly and focus on breath. (Repeat at teacher's discretion, for example, eight times, one minute, and so on.)

◆ MINDFUL LISTENING

This week's mindful listening exercises focus on sounds of nature, sounds from nonliving objects, and ambient sounds. These exercises can be done while seated, standing, or walking from one place to another. If using them during transition, try asking the questions at a stopping point along the way or when you reach your destination.

You'll find mindful listening scripts for each day this week on page 162.

◆ MINDFUL SEEING

This week's mindful seeing exercises focus on noticing shapes, sizes of objects, and colors. Like mindful listening, these exercises can be done while seated, standing, or walking from one place to another. If using them during transition, try asking the questions at a stopping point along the way or when you reach your destination.

You'll find mindful seeing scripts for each day this week on page 166.

◆ MINDFUL EATING

This week's mindful eating exercises focus on sense of touch, sense of sight, and sense of hearing. These exercises can be done during lunch or snack time. If you supply treats, be sure they come in a naturally small, individual form.

You'll find mindful eating scripts for each day this week on page 170.

As you review this week's mindfulness exercises on Friday, refresh everyone's memory on how to do the egg, caterpillar, chrysalis, and butterfly stretching poses. What new feelings do students notice as they do the poses again? When doing the other exercises, encourage students to make new observations. (For example, the theme of this week's poses is the life cycle of a butterfly. Ask students to reflect mindfully on their own life cycle so far.)

WEEK 30
SWAG Poses & Caring for the Earth

Mindful Eating

Suggested Week 30 Schedule

	MONDAY	TUESDAY	WEDNESDAY	THURSDAY	FRIDAY
Mindful Stretching	Snake	Waterfall	Astronaut	Gorilla	REVIEW
Mindful Breathing	Guided Breathing	Intentional Breathing	Guided Breathing	Intentional Breathing	Guided Breathing
Mindful Listening	Listen	Nature	Nonliving Objects	Humans	Listen
Mindful Seeing	See	Colors	Shapes	Sizes	See
Mindful Eating	Smell	Touch	Sight	Hear	Taste

MINDFUL STRETCHING—SWAG POSES ◇ ◇ ◇

SNAKE

1. Lie on your chest
2. Place your hands on the ground on each side of your head
3. Bring your elbows in close to your body
4. Lift up your chest
5. Take three deep breaths

WATERFALL

1. Stand with your feet slightly apart
2. Reach up with your hands
3. Look up
4. Lean back slightly
5. Take three deep breaths

ASTRONAUT

1. Stand with your feet together
2. Extend your arms to the side
3. Lift one leg and extend to the side
4. Take three deep breaths
5. Repeat with opposite side

GORILLA

1. Stand with your legs far apart
2. Extend your arms out to the side and make fists with your hands
3. Inhale and bring one fist to your chest
4. Exhale and extend that arm
5. Repeat with each arm three times

MINDFUL BREATHING

GUIDED BREATHING SEL TOPIC
Caring for the Earth (Monday/Wednesday/Friday)

We only have one Earth and it's ours to share with animals and other people. How have you taken care of Earth? What can you do to care for Earth today?

After a brief discussion about caring for Earth, continue with:

Sit cross-legged on the floor (or comfortably in your chair) with your hands on your knees. Relax your shoulders and close your eyes or look down. Breathe in and out through your nose. Now let's breathe together and think about what we can do to care for Earth.

Inhale . . . exhale . . . inhale . . . exhale . . . Continue to breathe slowly on your own. (Teacher chooses breathing length, for example, ten breaths, one minute, and so on.)

Slowly open your eyes or look up. Who would like to share about how they can care for Earth?

If students are slow to discuss their thoughts, get things started by sharing your own feelings. Continue the discussion as time allows.

INTENTIONAL BREATHING
"I Love Myself" (Tuesday/Thursday)

Today, we are going to say "I love myself" in our minds as we breathe. Close your eyes or look down. Relax your body and put your hands on your knees.

Slowly inhale and silently say "I love." Slowly exhale and silently say "myself."

Inhale "I love." Exhale "myself." (Repeat "I Love Myself" breathing at teacher's discretion, for example, eight times, one minute, and so on.)

◆ MINDFUL LISTENING

This week's mindful listening exercises focus on ambient sounds, sounds of nature, and sounds from nonliving objects. These exercises can be done while seated, standing, or walking from one place to another. If using them during transition, try asking the questions at a stopping point along the way or when you reach your destination.

You'll find mindful listening scripts for each day this week on page 162.

◆ MINDFUL SEEING

This week's mindful seeing exercises focus on noticing the immediate surroundings, noticing colors, and noticing shapes. Like mindful listening, these exercises can be done while seated, standing, or walking from one place to another. If using them during transition, try asking the questions at a stopping point along the way or when you reach your destination.

You'll find mindful seeing scripts for each day this week on page 166.

◆ MINDFUL EATING

This week's mindful eating exercises focus on sense of smell, sense of touch, and sense of sight. These exercises can be done during lunch or snack time. If you supply treats, be sure they come in a naturally small, individual form.

You'll find mindful eating scripts for each day this week on page 170.

Allow students extra time today for Friday review, prompting them to share something they've learned from their mindful observations this week. Refresh everyone's memory on how to do the snake, waterfall, astronaut, and gorilla stretching poses. What new feelings do students notice as they do the poses again? When doing the other exercises, encourage students to make new observations. (For example, extend the discussion about caring for the earth and ask students to suggest one way to care for the earth based on how they mindfully listened to nature.)

WEEK 31
Plant Poses & Taking Responsibility

Mindful Breathing

Suggested Week 31 Schedule

	MONDAY	TUESDAY	WEDNESDAY	THURSDAY	FRIDAY
Mindful Stretching	Sun	Soil	Waterfall	Plant	REVIEW
Mindful Breathing	Guided Breathing	Intentional Breathing	Guided Breathing	Intentional Breathing	Guided Breathing
Mindful Listening	Listen	Nature	Nonliving Objects	Humans	Listen
Mindful Seeing	See	Colors	Shapes	Sizes	See
Mindful Eating	Smell	Touch	Sight	Hear	Taste

MINDFUL STRETCHING—PLANT POSES ◆ ◆ ◆

SUN

1. Stand with your feet together
2. Extend your arms to the side with palms facing up
3. Gently lean back and look up
4. Take three deep breaths

SOIL

1. Lie on your back with your arms and legs flat
2. Palms facing up
3. Close your eyes
4. Take three deep breaths

WATERFALL

1. Stand with your feet slightly apart
2. Reach up with your hands
3. Look up
4. Lean back slightly
5. Take three deep breaths

PLANT

1. Stand with your feet together
2. Extend your arms up diagonally
3. Smile big
4. Take three deep breaths

MINDFUL BREATHING ◇ ◇ ◇ ◇ ◇ ◇ ◇ ◇

GUIDED BREATHING SEL TOPIC
Taking Responsibility (Monday/Wednesday/Friday)

It's important to take responsibility for our actions and not blame others for our decisions. When have you taken responsibility? How can you take responsibility today?

After a brief discussion about taking responsibility, continue with:
Sit cross-legged on the floor (or comfortably in your chair) with your hands on your knees. Relax your shoulders and close your eyes or look down. Breathe in and out through your nose. Now let's breathe together and think about taking responsibility for our actions.

Inhale . . . exhale . . . inhale . . . exhale . . . Continue to breathe slowly on your own. (Teacher chooses breathing length, for example, ten breaths, one minute, and so on.)

Slowly open your eyes or look up. Who would like to share about taking responsibility for their actions?

If students are slow to discuss their thoughts, get things started by sharing your own feelings. Continue the discussion as time allows.

◇ ◇ ◇ ◇ ◇ ◇ ◇ ◇ ◇ ◇ ◇ ◇ ◇ ◇

INTENTIONAL BREATHING
Nose Breathing (Tuesday/Thursday)

Today, we are going to do nose breathing. Close your eyes or look down. Relax your body and put your hands on your knees.

Slowly inhale through your *nose* and hold for three seconds. Slowly exhale through your *nose*.

Inhale and hold for three seconds. Exhale slowly. (Repeat nose breathing at teacher's discretion, for example, eight times, one minute, and so on.)

◆ MINDFUL LISTENING

This week's mindful listening exercises focus on human sounds, nonliving sounds, and sounds from nearby surroundings. These exercises can be done while seated, standing, or walking from one place to another. If using them during transition, try asking the questions at a stopping point along the way or when you reach your destination.

You'll find mindful listening scripts for each day this week on page 162.

◆ MINDFUL SEEING

This week's mindful seeing exercises focus on noticing sizes of objects, noticing colors, and noticing the immediate surroundings. Like mindful listening, these exercises can be done while seated, standing, or walking from one place to another. If using them during transition, try asking the questions at a stopping point along the way or when you reach your destination.

You'll find mindful seeing scripts for each day this week on page 166.

◆ MINDFUL EATING

This week's mindful eating exercises focus on sense of hearing, sense of taste, and sense of touch. These exercises can be done during lunch or snack time. If you supply treats, be sure they come in a naturally small, individual form.

You'll find mindful eating scripts for each day this week on page 170.

Friday review should be a happy occasion. Make it a celebration of the week's mindful accomplishments. Ask for volunteers to lead the exercises. Refresh everyone's memory on how to do the sun, soil, waterfall, and plant stretching poses. What new feelings do students notice as they do the poses again? When doing the other exercises, encourage students to make new observations. (For example, ask students to reflect on what they've learned about their food after mindfully eating.)

WEEK 32
LIFE Poses & Being a Team Player

Mindful Stretching

Suggested Week 32 Schedule

	MONDAY	TUESDAY	WEDNESDAY	THURSDAY	FRIDAY
Mindful Stretching	Locust	Igloo	Frog	Elephant	REVIEW
Mindful Breathing	Guided Breathing	Intentional Breathing	Guided Breathing	Intentional Breathing	Guided Breathing
Mindful Listening	Listen	Nature	Nonliving Objects	Humans	Listen
Mindful Seeing	See	Colors	Shapes	Sizes	See
Mindful Eating	Smell	Touch	Sight	Hear	Taste

MINDFUL STRETCHING—LIFE POSES ◊   ◊   ◊   ◊

LOCUST

1. Lie on your chest
2. Extend your arms in front of you
3. Lift your arms and legs
4. Take three deep breaths

IGLOO

1. Start on your knees
2. Sit back on your heels and gently bring your forehead to the ground
3. Rest your arms alongside your legs
4. Take three deep breaths

FROG

1. Stand with your feet shoulder-width apart
2. Looking forward, squat down close to the ground
3. Put your hands on the ground between your legs
4. Take three deep breaths

ELEPHANT

1. Stand with your feet shoulder-width apart
2. Bend at your waist, look down, and grasp your hands together
3. Inhale slowly and sway to one side
4. Exhale slowly and sway to the other side
5. Repeat three times

MINDFUL BREATHING ◇ ◇ ◇ ◇ ◇ ◇ ◇ ◇

GUIDED BREATHING SEL TOPIC
Being a Team Player (Monday/Wednesday/Friday)

Teams aren't just for sports. Together Everyone Achieves More is an acronym for TEAM. When have you been a team player? How can you be a team player today?

After a brief discussion about being a team player, continue with:

Sit cross-legged on the floor (or comfortably in your chair) with your hands on your knees. Relax your shoulders and close your eyes or look down. Breathe in and out through your nose. Now let's breathe together and think about how we can be a team player.

Inhale . . . exhale . . . inhale . . . exhale . . . Continue to breathe slowly on your own. (Teacher chooses breathing length, for example, ten breaths, one minute, and so on.)

Slowly open your eyes or look up. Who would like to share about how they can be a team player?

If students are slow to discuss their thoughts, get things started by sharing your own feelings. Continue the discussion as time allows.

◇ ◇ ◇ ◇ ◇ ◇ ◇ ◇ ◇ ◇ ◇ ◇ ◇ ◇

INTENTIONAL BREATHING
"I Am Strong" (Tuesday/Thursday)

Today, we are going to say "I am strong" in our minds as we breathe. Close your eyes or look down. Relax your body and put your hands on your knees.

Slowly inhale and silently say "I am." Slowly exhale and silently say "strong."

Inhale "I am." Exhale "strong." (Repeat "I Am Strong" breathing at teacher's discretion, for example, eight times, one minute, and so on.)

◆ MINDFUL LISTENING

This week's mindful listening exercises focus on sounds of nature, sounds from nonliving objects, and ambient sounds. These exercises can be done while seated, standing, or walking from one place to another. If using them during transition, try asking the questions at a stopping point along the way or when you reach your destination.

You'll find mindful listening scripts for each day this week on page 162.

◆ MINDFUL SEEING

This week's mindful seeing exercises focus on noticing shapes, sizes of objects, and colors. Like mindful listening, these exercises can be done while seated, standing, or walking from one place to another. If using them during transition, try asking the questions at a stopping point along the way or when you reach your destination.

You'll find mindful seeing scripts for each day this week on page 166.

◆ MINDFUL EATING

This week's mindful eating exercises focus on sense of touch, sense of sight, and sense of hearing. These exercises can be done during lunch or snack time. If you supply treats, be sure they come in a naturally small, individual form.

You'll find mindful eating scripts for each day this week on page 170.

By now, spring is (hopefully) showing sides outside. Make your Friday review spring-themed. Maybe take the class outside or ask everyone to draw flowers to liven up the classroom. Refresh everyone's memory on how to do the locust, igloo, frog, and elephant stretching poses. What new feelings do students notice as they do the poses again? When doing the other exercises, encourage students to make new observations. (For example, ask students to choose a topic for a guided breathing exercise. How can they make it a mindful exercise?)

WEEK 33
PLAY Poses & Put-Downs

Mindful Listening

Suggested Week 33 Schedule

	MONDAY	TUESDAY	WEDNESDAY	THURSDAY	FRIDAY
Mindful Stretching	Plank	Lion	Astronaut	Yawn	REVIEW
Mindful Breathing	Guided Breathing	Intentional Breathing	Guided Breathing	Intentional Breathing	Guided Breathing
Mindful Listening	Listen	Nature	Nonliving Objects	Humans	Listen
Mindful Seeing	See	Colors	Shapes	Sizes	See
Mindful Eating	Smell	Touch	Sight	Hear	Taste

MINDFUL STRETCHING—PLAY POSES ◇   ◇   ◇   ◇

PLANK

1. Lie on your chest
2. Place your hands near your shoulders
3. Push your body off the ground so you're on your hands and your toes are flexed
4. Keep your body in a diagonal line
5. Take three deep breaths

LION

1. Start on your knees
2. Sit back on your heels
3. Place your hands on your knees
4. Take three deep lion breaths

ASTRONAUT

1. Stand with your feet together
2. Extend your arms to the side
3. Lift one leg and extend to the side
4. Take three deep breaths
5. Repeat with opposite side

YAWN

1. Stand with feet together
2. Extend arms diagonally
3. Inhale slowly
4. Exhale with a big yawn and stretch
5. Repeat three times

MINDFUL BREATHING ◇ ◇ ◇ ◇ ◇ ◇ ◇ ◇

GUIDED BREATHING SEL TOPIC
Put-Downs (Monday/Wednesday/Friday)

Use your words to stand up for yourself and others when put-downs happen. When have you dealt with a put-down? How can you handle put-downs in a peaceful manner?

After a brief discussion about put-downs, continue with:

Sit cross-legged on the floor (or comfortably in your chair) with your hands on your knees. Relax your shoulders and close your eyes or look down. Breathe in and out through your nose. Now let's breathe together and think about how we can handle put downs.

Inhale . . . exhale . . . inhale . . . exhale . . . Continue to breathe slowly on your own. (Teacher chooses breathing length, for example, ten breaths, one minute, and so on.)

Slowly open your eyes or look up. Who would like to share about how they can handle put-downs?

If students are slow to discuss their thoughts, get things started by sharing your own feelings. Continue the discussion as time allows.

◇ ◇ ◇ ◇ ◇ ◇ ◇ ◇ ◇ ◇ ◇ ◇ ◇ ◇

INTENTIONAL BREATHING
Nose-Mouth Breathing (Tuesday/Thursday)

Today, we are going to do nose-mouth breathing. Close your eyes or look down. Relax your body and put your hands on your knees.

Slowly inhale through your *nose* and hold for three seconds. Slowly exhale through your *mouth*.

Inhale and hold for three seconds. Exhale slowly. (Repeat inhale-exhale at teacher's discretion, for example, eight times, one minute, and so on.)

◆ MINDFUL LISTENING

This week's mindful listening exercises focus on ambient sounds, sounds of nature, and sounds from nonliving objects. These exercises can be done while seated, standing, or walking from one place to another. If using them during transition, try asking the questions at a stopping point along the way or when you reach your destination.

You'll find mindful listening scripts for each day this week on page 162.

◆ MINDFUL SEEING

This week's mindful seeing exercises focus on noticing the immediate surroundings, noticing colors, and noticing shapes. Like mindful listening, these exercises can be done while seated, standing, or walking from one place to another. If using them during transition, try asking the questions at a stopping point along the way or when you reach your destination.

You'll find mindful seeing scripts for each day this week on page 166.

◆ MINDFUL EATING

This week's mindful eating exercises focus on sense of smell, sense of touch, and sense of sight. These exercises can be done during lunch or snack time. If you supply treats, be sure they come in a naturally small, individual form.

You'll find mindful eating scripts for each day this week on page 170.

Friday review is second nature by now. Add a few surprises today: Reverse the order of the stretching poses, add more time to the breathing exercises, and so on. Refresh everyone's memory on how to do the plank, lion, astronaut, and yawn stretching poses. What new feelings do students notice as they do the poses again? When doing the other exercises, encourage students to make new observations. (For example, extend the discussion of put-downs and create a class list of ways to help someone who has been put down.)

WEEK 34
SWIM Poses & Trying Your Best

Mindful Seeing

Suggested Week 34 Schedule

	MONDAY	TUESDAY	WEDNESDAY	THURSDAY	FRIDAY
Mindful Stretching	Snake	Waterfall	Igloo	Mountain Top	REVIEW
Mindful Breathing	Guided Breathing	Intentional Breathing	Guided Breathing	Intentional Breathing	Guided Breathing
Mindful Listening	Listen	Nature	Nonliving Objects	Humans	Listen
Mindful Seeing	See	Colors	Shapes	Sizes	See
Mindful Eating	Smell	Touch	Sight	Hear	Taste

MINDFUL STRETCHING—SWIM POSES ◇   ◇   ◇

SNAKE

1. Lie on your chest
2. Place your hands on the ground on each side of your head
3. Bring your elbows in close to your body
4. Lift up your chest
5. Take three deep breaths

WATERFALL

1. Stand with your feet slightly apart
2. Reach up with your hands
3. Look up
4. Lean back slightly
5. Take three deep breaths

IGLOO

1. Start on your knees
2. Sit back on your heels and gently bring your forehead to the ground
3. Rest your arms alongside your legs
4. Take three deep breaths

MOUNTAIN TOP

1. Stand with your feet together
2. Extend your arms above your head
3. Place your palms together
4. Take three deep breaths

MINDFUL BREATHING

GUIDED BREATHING SEL TOPIC
Trying Your Best (Monday/Wednesday/Thursday)

Always try your best. No matter what. Nothing is possible if you don't try. When have you tried your best? What is a situation where you can try your best?

After a brief discussion about trying your best, continue with:

Sit cross-legged on the floor (or comfortably in your chair) with your hands on your knees. Relax your shoulders and close your eyes or look down. Breathe in and out through your nose. Now let's breathe together and think about trying our best.

Inhale . . . exhale . . . inhale . . . exhale . . . Continue to breathe slowly on your own. (Teacher chooses breathing length, for example, ten breaths, one minute, and so on.)

Slowly open your eyes or look up. Who would like to share about how they can try their best?

If students are slow to discuss their thoughts, get things started by sharing your own feelings. Continue the discussion as time allows.

◊ ◊ ◊ ◊ ◊ ◊ ◊ ◊ ◊ ◊ ◊ ◊ ◊ ◊

INTENTIONAL BREATHING
"I Am Kind" (Tuesday/Thursday)

Today, we are going to say "I am kind" in our minds as we breathe. Close your eyes or look down. Relax your body and put your hands on your knees.

Slowly inhale and silently say "I am." Slowly exhale and silently say "kind."

Inhale "I am." Exhale "kind." (Repeat "I Am Kind" breathing at teacher's discretion, for example, eight times, one minute, and so on.)

◆ MINDFUL LISTENING

This week's mindful listening exercises focus on human sounds, nonliving sounds, and sounds from nearby surroundings. These exercises can be done while seated, standing, or walking from one place to another. If using them during transition, try asking the questions at a stopping point along the way or when you reach your destination.

You'll find mindful listening scripts for each day this week on page 162.

◆ MINDFUL SEEING

This week's mindful seeing exercises focus on noticing sizes of objects, noticing colors, and noticing the immediate surroundings. Like mindful listening, these exercises can be done while seated, standing, or walking from one place to another. If using them during transition, try asking the questions at a stopping point along the way or when you reach your destination.

You'll find mindful seeing scripts for each day this week on page 166.

◆ MINDFUL EATING

This week's mindful eating exercises focus on sense of hearing, sense of taste, and sense of touch. These exercises can be done during lunch or snack time. If you supply treats, be sure they come in a naturally small, individual form.

You'll find mindful eating scripts for each day this week on page 170.

Fridays should not only be a day of review but also a day to acknowledge accomplishments. Note the progress everyone has made over the course of the year when it comes to mindfulness. Refresh everyone's memory on how to do the snake, waterfall, igloo, and mountain top stretching poses. What new feelings do students notice as they do the poses again? When doing the other exercises, encourage students to make new observations. (For example, ask students about objects they've been able to both see and hear mindfully and what they noticed.)

WEEK 35
Summer Poses & Having Fun

Mindful Eating

Suggested Week 35 Schedule

	MONDAY	TUESDAY	WEDNESDAY	THURSDAY	FRIDAY
Mindful Stretching	Relax	Ice Cream	Swim	Daydream	REVIEW
Mindful Breathing	Guided Breathing	Intentional Breathing	Guided Breathing	Intentional Breathing	Guided Breathing
Mindful Listening	Listen	Nature	Nonliving Objects	Humans	Listen
Mindful Seeing	See	Colors	Shapes	Sizes	See
Mindful Eating	Smell	Touch	Sight	Hear	Taste

MINDFUL STRETCHING—SUMMER POSES ◇ ◇ ◇

RELAX

1. Sit cross-legged
2. Put your hands on your knees
3. Close your eyes
4. Take three deep breaths

ICE CREAM

1. Stand with feet shoulder-width apart
2. Bend your knees and squat down
3. Bring your arms in front of you
4. Bend elbows and grasp hands together pretending to hold an ice-cream cone
5. Take three deep breaths

SWIM

1. Lie on your chest
2. Lift one arm and your opposite leg (R-L) off the ground
3. Take three deep breaths
4. Repeat with opposite side

DAYDREAM

1. Lie on your back with your arms and legs flat
2. Palms down
3. Close your eyes
4. Take three deep breaths

MINDFUL BREATHING

GUIDED BREATHING SEL TOPIC
Having Fun (Monday/Wednesday/Friday)

Have fun. Smile. Enjoy yourself. Life is way more enjoyable when you're having fun. What is a time when you had fun? How can you have fun today?

After a brief discussion about having fun, continue with:

Sit cross-legged on the floor (or comfortably in your chair) with your hands on your knees. Relax your shoulders and close your eyes or look down. Breathe in and out through your nose. Now let's breathe together and think about having fun.

Inhale . . . exhale . . . inhale . . . exhale . . . Continue to breathe slowly on your own. (Teacher chooses breathing length, for example, ten breaths, one minute, and so on.)

Slowly open your eyes or look up. Who would like to share about having fun?

If students are slow to discuss their thoughts, get things started by sharing your own feelings. Continue the discussion as time allows.

INTENTIONAL BREATHING
Focus on the Breath (Tuesday/Thursday)

Today, we are going to focus on the breath. Close your eyes or look down. Relax your body and put your hands on your knees.

Slowly inhale and focus on breath filling your lungs. Slowly exhale and focus on breath leaving your body.

Inhale slowly and focus on breath. Exhale slowly and focus on breath. (Repeat at teacher's discretion, for example, eight times, one minute, and so on.)

◆ MINDFUL LISTENING

This week's mindful listening exercises focus on sounds of nature, sounds from nonliving objects, and ambient sounds. These exercises can be done while seated, standing, or walking from one place to another. If using them during transition, try asking the questions at a stopping point along the way or when you reach your destination.

You'll find mindful listening scripts for each day this week on page 162.

◆ MINDFUL SEEING

This week's mindful seeing exercises focus on noticing shapes, sizes of objects, and colors. Like mindful listening, these exercises can be done while seated, standing, or walking from one place to another. If using them during transition, try asking the questions at a stopping point along the way or when you reach your destination.

You'll find mindful seeing scripts for each day this week on page 166.

◆ MINDFUL EATING

This week's mindful eating exercises focus on sense of touch, sense of sight, and sense of hearing. These exercises can be done during lunch or snack time. If you supply treats, be sure they come in a naturally small, individual form.

You'll find mindful eating scripts for each day this week on page 170.

Summer is so close you can taste it (mindfully, of course). Friday review is a chance to revel in success and be mindful of the path it took to get here. Refresh everyone's memory on how to do the relax, ice cream, swim, and daydream stretching poses. What new feelings do students notice as they do the poses again? When doing the other exercises, encourage students to make new observations. (For example, extend the discussion of having fun and how students might use their mindfulness skills during summer vacation.)

WEEK 36
Student Choice & Taking It Home

Mindful Breathing

Suggested Week 36 Schedule

	MONDAY	TUESDAY	WEDNESDAY	THURSDAY	FRIDAY
Mindful Stretching	STUDENT CHOICE	STUDENT CHOICE	STUDENT CHOICE	STUDENT CHOICE	REVIEW
Mindful Breathing	Guided Breathing	Intentional Breathing	Guided Breathing	Intentional Breathing	Guided Breathing
Mindful Listening	Listen	Nature	Nonliving Objects	Humans	Listen
Mindful Seeing	See	Colors	Shapes	Sizes	See
Mindful Eating	Smell	Touch	Sight	Hear	Taste

MINDFUL STRETCHING—STUDENT CHOICE

Allow students to choose poses from the previous eight weeks (or any poses since the beginning of the school year) or to create their own poses. Ask students who create new poses to teach their poses to the class.

MINDFUL BREATHING ◇ ◇ ◇ ◇ ◇ ◇ ◇ ◇

GUIDED BREATHING SEL TOPIC
Taking It Home (Monday/Wednesday/Friday)

66 **We've learned about a lot this year. Even though we learned about it in a classroom, it all applies to life. What lessons have you used outside class? What lessons do you plan on using?**

After a brief discussion about what lessons students have used, continue with: **Sit cross-legged on the floor (or comfortably in your chair) with your hands on your knees. Relax your shoulders and close your eyes or look down. Breathe in and out through your nose. Now let's breathe together and think about how you plan on using these lessons at home.**

Inhale . . . exhale . . . inhale . . . exhale . . . Continue to breathe slowly on your own. (Teacher chooses breathing length, for example, ten breaths, one minute, and so on.)

Slowly open your eyes or look up. Who would like to share about what you plan to use at home?

If students are slow to discuss their thoughts, get things started by sharing your own feelings. Continue the discussion as time allows.

◇ ◇ ◇ ◇ ◇ ◇ ◇ ◇ ◇ ◇ ◇ ◇ ◇ ◇ ◇

INTENTIONAL BREATHING
"I Love Myself" (Tuesday/Thursday)

66 **Today, we are going to say "I love myself" in our minds as we breathe. Close your eyes or look down. Relax your body and put your hands on your knees.**

Slowly inhale and silently say "I love." Slowly exhale and silently say "myself."

Inhale "I love." Exhale "myself." (Repeat "I Love Myself" breathing at teacher's discretion, for example, eight times, one minute, and so on.)

◆ MINDFUL LISTENING

This week's mindful listening exercises focus on ambient sounds, sounds of nature, and sounds from nonliving objects. These exercises can be done while seated, standing, or walking from one place to another. If using them during transition, try asking the questions at a stopping point along the way or when you reach your destination.

You'll find mindful listening scripts for each day this week on page 162.

◆ MINDFUL SEEING

This week's mindful seeing exercises focus on noticing the immediate surroundings, noticing colors, and noticing shapes. Like mindful listening, these exercises can be done while seated, standing, or walking from one place to another. If using them during transition, try asking the questions at a stopping point along the way or when you reach your destination.

You'll find mindful seeing scripts for each day this week on page 166.

◆ MINDFUL EATING

This week's mindful eating exercises focus on sense of smell, sense of touch, and sense of sight. These exercises can be done during lunch or snack time. If you supply treats, be sure they come in a naturally small, individual form.

You'll find mindful eating scripts for each day this week on page 170.

Celebrate, celebrate, celebrate! The final Friday review is here. Have a classroom discussion of all the stretching poses students have learned this year. Refresh their memory of the ones they've learned during the last nine weeks. As a group, choose five poses to review together. What new feelings do students notice as they do the poses again? When doing the other exercises, encourage students to make new observations. (For example, ask students if and how they've noticed any changes to the way they listen now that they can listen mindfully.)

ACKNOWLEDGMENTS

My 2015–2016 preK class: the Bubbles (featured in chapter opening photos)

All of my preK and K classes: Rainbows, Sharks, Snowpeople, Snakes, Buckeyes, Spongebobs, Rhinos, Spiders, Jaguars, Doggy Dogs, and Bow Wows

Gullett Elementary School (Austin, TX) and Janie Ruiz, principal

Piloting teachers: Jessica Rodriguez, Missy Russell, Kimberly Davishines, Melissa Goodwin, Gilberto Ferrer, Alyssa Absher, Joanna Fairbrother, Allison Hinojosa, Jeanine Frenzel, Betsey Marischen, Stephani Kyler, Elia Simons, Marjorie Bennett, Molly Nikle

Austin Independent School District and Dr. Paul Cruz, superintendent

Photographer: Stephanie Friedman

Logo design: Bryony Gomez-Palacio, Under Consideration, LLC

Lawyers: Phil Russ and Brian Buster

Videographer: Justin Browne

Business advisor: Piper Browne

Kickstarter Stars: Ryan Newman, Tom & Mefide Geretz, Scott Beardslee, Cindy Anderson, Stella Maxwell, Spilled Milk Social Club, Katy Livingston, Andy Lahman, Randy Deeks, Lee & Mary Deeks, Nate & Megan Little, Jenifer & Gregg DeAtley, David & Karen Schmidt, Mattie Clark, Lindsay Jo, Kalie Virden, Haley & Matt Wagoner, Steve & Mary Wagoner, Susan Biles & Mike Nink, Daniel Zarakov & Stefano Meschiari, Elizabeth & Michael Bomba, Tamas O'Doughda, Alec & April Rose, Keith Sweigert, Mike & Michele Horn, Carol & Paul Nye, Ben & Steph Geletka, Lauren Price, David Lee, Doris O'Brien, Isaac Marischen, Betsey & Mike Marischen, Heather Christian Drew, Jules & Mark Overly, Nate & Rach Waas Shull, Rey Cardenas, Practice Yoga Austin, Carlee Wineholt, Andres Bueker, Nancy & Bob Rigney, Aimee & Brad Olivier, Beth & Kevin McHorse, Amy & Phil Russ, Kyle Fisher & Abby Comeau, Jackie Strong & Gary Meyer, O.W. Bussey (Deontré), Buddy Tom Rosen, Paige Melvin, Paul Schlaud, Amy & Jason Williams, Jenn Nolan Boerio, Lon Allen, Ryan Linstromberg, Stacey Urps

Kickstarter Superstars: Macey & Bryan Garwood, Mary Ellen Isaacs, Adam Longacre, Laura Beck & Brendon Cahoon, Leslie & Lee Johnson, Jane & Mike Cahoon, Jean & Tom Butler, Kathy Wineholt, Craig & Stephanie Normand, Gus Davis

Kickstarter All-Stars: Kathy & Joe Long, Mike Vajentic, Steve & Sherron Barnes

Kickstarter GOATs (Greatest of All Time): Jim Heighway, Dr. Wayne Bockmon, Aaron Lahman & Sara Leoni, Amy Laug, Walnut Street School (Iowa), Grandma Butler (Joan), Grandpa Butler (Ed), Lindsay Harris

ENDNOTES

1. Antoine Lutz, Heleen A. Slagter, John D. Dunne, and Richard J. Davidson, "Attention Regulation and Monitoring in Mediation." *Trends in Cognitive Science* 12 (4), (2008), 163–169.

2. Alberto Chiesa and Alessandro Serretti, "A Systematic Review of Neurobiological and Clinical Features of Mindfulness Meditations." *Psychological Medicine* 40 (8), (2010), 1239–1252.

3. Philippe R. Goldin and James J. Gross, "Effects of Mindfulness-Based Stress Reduction (MBSR) on Emotion Regulation in Social Anxiety Disorder." *Emotion* 10 (1), (2010), 83–91.

4. Michael D. Mrazek et al. "Mindfulness Training Improves Working Memory Capacity and GRE Performance While Reducing Mind Wandering." *Psychological Science* 24 (5), (2013), 776–781.

5. David S. Black and Randima Fernando. "Mindfulness Training and Classroom Behavior Among Lower-Income and Ethnic Minority Elementary School Children." *Journal of Child and Family Studies* 23 (7), (2014), 1242–1246.

6. William Kuyken et al. "Effectiveness of the Mindfulness in Schools Programme: Non-Randomised Controlled Feasibility Study." *The British Journal of Psychiatry* 203 (2), (2013), 126–131.

APPENDIX
Mindfulness Exercise Scripts

The scripts for each mindfulness exercise (breathing, listening, seeing, eating) are included here. Feel free to reproduce these pages to have the scripts readily available. To print out these pages, see page 181 for instructions on how to download.

MINDFUL BREATHING SCRIPTS ◊ ◊ ◊ ◊ ◊ ◊

GENERAL GUIDED BREATHING SCRIPT

Sit cross-legged on the floor (or comfortably in your chair) with your hands on your knees. Relax your shoulders and close your eyes or look down. Breathe in and out through your nose. Now let's breathe together.

Inhale . . . exhale . . . inhale . . . exhale . . . Continue to breathe slowly on your own. (Teacher chooses breathing length, for example, ten breaths, one minute, and so on.)

Slowly open your eyes or look up. Who would like to share how they feel?

NOSE BREATHING

Today, we are going to do nose breathing. Close your eyes or look down. Relax your body and put your hands on your knees.

Slowly inhale through your *nose* and hold for three seconds. One . . . two . . . three . . . Slowly exhale through your *nose*.

Inhale and hold for three seconds. One . . . two . . . three . . . Exhale slowly. (Repeat inhale-exhale at teacher's discretion, for example, eight times, one minute, and so on.)

NOSE-MOUTH BREATHING

Today, we are going to do nose-mouth breathing. Close your eyes or look down. Relax your body and put your hands on your knees.

Slowly inhale through your *nose* and hold for three seconds. Slowly exhale through your *mouth*.

Inhale and hold for three seconds. Exhale slowly. (Repeat inhale-exhale at teacher's discretion, for example, eight times, one minute, and so on.)

FOCUS ON THE BREATH

Today, we are going to focus on the breath. Close your eyes or look down. Relax your body and put your hands on your knees.

Slowly inhale and focus on breath filling your lungs. Slowly exhale and focus on breath leaving your body.

Inhale slowly and focus on breath. Exhale slowly and focus on breath. (Repeat at teacher's discretion, for example, eight times, one minute, and so on.)

"I AM STRONG" BREATHING

Today, we are going to say "I am strong" in our minds as we breathe. Close your eyes or look down. Relax your body and put your hands on your knees.

Slowly inhale and silently say "I am." Slowly exhale and silently say "strong."

Inhale "I am." Exhale "strong." (Repeat "I Am Strong" breathing at teacher's discretion, for example, eight times, one minute, and so on.)

"I LOVE MYSELF" BREATHING

Today, we are going to say "I love myself" in our minds as we breathe. Close your eyes or look down. Relax your body and put your hands on your knees.

Slowly inhale and silently say "I love." Slowly exhale and silently say "myself."

Inhale "I love." Exhale "myself." (Repeat "I Love Myself" breathing at teacher's discretion, for example, eight times, one minute, and so on.)

"I AM KIND" BREATHING

Today, we are going to say "I am kind" in our minds as we breathe. Close your eyes or look down. Relax your body and put your hands on your knees.

Slowly inhale and silently say "I am." Slowly exhale and silently say "kind."

Inhale "I am." Exhale "kind." (Repeat "I Am Kind" breathing at teacher's discretion, for example, eight times, one minute, and so on.)

MINDFUL LISTENING SCRIPTS ◇ ◇ ◇ ◇ ◇ ◇ ◇

USE FOR WEEKS 1–36

MONDAY

Objective: To encourage students to be aware of their surroundings and practice being in the moment.

- These exercises can be done while seated, standing, or walking from one place to another.
- If using them during transition, try asking the questions at a stopping point along the way or when you reach your destination.

❝ **Today for mindful listening, we are going to focus on noticing sounds in our surroundings. We don't have to name the sounds. We're just going to practice noticing sounds. Mindful listening is a great strategy to help you when you feel like you might need some calm.**

Turn your attention to the sounds around you. What do you notice? Silently acknowledge the different and subtle sounds that you hear. Just notice them. If other thoughts arise, gently acknowledge the thoughts, take a deep breath, and return your attention to the sounds you can hear. Let's begin.

Set a timer for one minute. As your students grow more experienced at mindful listening, increase the time increments gradually over the course of the year. When time's up, have a conversation with your students using these questions:

- **What did you notice from that experience?**
- **What was it like to intentionally listen to and notice sounds?**
- **Did you notice different sounds?**
- **If so, what was different about the sounds?**

Continue the conversation as time allow.

TUESDAY

Objective: To encourage students to be aware of their surroundings and practice being in the moment.

- These exercises can be done while seated, standing, or walking from one place to another.
- If using them during transition, try asking the questions at a stopping point along the way or when you reach your destination.
- If you don't have access to the outdoors and nature sounds, you can find plenty of clips on YouTube.

" Today for mindful listening, we are going to focus on noticing sounds of nature in this moment. Mindful listening is a great strategy to help you when you feel like you might need some calm.

Turn your attention to the sounds around you. What nature sounds do you notice? Silently acknowledge the different and subtle nature sounds that you hear. If other thoughts arise, gently acknowledge the thoughts, take a deep breath, and return your attention to the nature sounds you can hear. Let's begin.

After the allotted time (one to five minutes), have a conversation with your students using these questions:

- **What did you notice from that experience?**
- **What was it like to intentionally listen to and notice sounds of nature?**
- **Did you notice different sounds?**
- **If so, what different sounds did you notice?**

Continue the discussion as time allows.

WEDNESDAY

Objective: To encourage students to be aware of their surroundings and practice being in the moment.

- These exercises can be done while seated, standing, or walking from one place to another.
- If using them during transition, try asking the questions at a stopping point along the way or when you reach your destination.

" Today for mindful listening, we are going to focus on noticing sounds of nonliving objects in this moment. Mindful listening is a great strategy to help you when you feel like you might need some calm.

Turn your attention to the sounds around you. What nonliving object sounds do you notice? Silently acknowledge the different and subtle nonliving object sounds that you hear. If other thoughts arise, gently acknowledge the thoughts, take a deep breath, and return your attention to the nonliving object sounds you can hear. Let's begin.

After the allotted time (one to five minutes), have a conversation with your students using these questions:

- **What did you notice from that experience?**
- **What was it like to intentionally listen to and notice sounds of nonliving objects?**
- **Did you notice different sounds?**
- **If so, what different sounds did you notice?**

Continue the discussion for as long as time allows.

THURSDAY

Objective: To encourage students to be aware of their surroundings and practice being in the moment.

- These exercises can be done while seated, standing, or walking from one place to another.
- If using them during transition, try asking the questions at a stopping point along the way or when you reach your destination.

Today for mindful listening, we are going to focus on noticing human sounds in this moment. Mindful listening is a great strategy to help you when you feel like you might need some calm.

Turn your attention to the sounds around you. Without making loud intentional sounds ourselves, what human sounds do you notice? Silently acknowledge the different and subtle human sounds that you hear. If other thoughts arise, gently acknowledge the thoughts, take a deep breath, and return your attention to the human sounds you can hear. Let's begin.

After the allotted time (one to five minutes), have a conversation with your students using these questions:

- **What did you notice from that experience?**
- **What was it like to intentionally listen to and notice sounds?**
- **Did you notice different sounds?**
- **If so, what different sounds did you notice?**

Continue the discussion as time allows.

FRIDAY

Objective: To encourage students to be aware of their surroundings and practice being in the moment.

- These exercises can be done while seated, standing, or walking from one place to another.
- If using them during transition, try asking the questions at a stopping point along the way or when you reach your destination.

"

Today for mindful listening, we are going to focus on noticing sounds in our surroundings. We don't have to name the sounds. We're just going to practice noticing sounds. Mindful listening is a great strategy to help you when you feel like you might need some calm.

Turn your attention to the sounds around you. What do you notice? Silently acknowledge the different and subtle sounds that you hear. There's no need to name these sounds. Just notice them. If other thoughts arise, gently acknowledge the thoughts, take a deep breath, and return your attention to the sounds you can hear. Let's begin.

After the allotted time (one to five minutes), have a conversation with your students using these questions:

- **What did you notice from that experience?**
- **What was it like to intentionally listen to and notice sounds?**
- **Did you notice different sounds?**
- **If so, what different sounds did you notice?**

Continue the discussion as time allows.

MINDFUL SEEING SCRIPTS ◇ ◇ ◇ ◇ ◇ ◇ ◇

USE FOR WEEKS 1–36

MONDAY

Objective: To encourage students to be aware of their surroundings and practice being in the moment.

- These exercises can be done while seated, standing, or walking from one place to another.
- If using them during transition, try asking the questions at a stopping point along the way or when you reach your destination.

Today for mindful seeing, we are going to focus on noticing our surroundings with our eyes. We don't have to name what we see. We're just going to practice noticing. Mindful seeing is a good way to help you when you feel like you might need some calm.

Turn your attention to the sights around you. What do you notice? Silently acknowledge the different and subtle things that you see. Just notice them. If other thoughts arise, gently acknowledge the thoughts, take a deep breath, and return your attention to the things you can see.

Set a timer for one minute. As your students grow more experienced at mindful seeing, increase the time increments gradually over the course of the year. When time's up, have a conversation with your students using these questions:

- **What did you notice from that experience?**
- **What was it like to intentionally look at and notice your surroundings?**
- **Did you notice different things?**
- **If so, what was different about the things you saw?**

Continue the discussion as time allows.

TUESDAY

Objective: To encourage students to be aware of their surroundings and practice being in the moment.

- These exercises can be done while seated, standing, or walking from one place to another.
- If using them during transition, try asking the questions at a stopping point along the way or when you reach your destination.

Today for mindful seeing, we are going to focus on noticing colors. The purpose of this exercise is to help us notice colors in our surroundings in the

present moment. Mindful seeing is a great strategy to help you when you feel like you might need some calm.

Turn your attention to the sights around you. What colors do you notice? Silently acknowledge the different colors that you see. If other thoughts arise, gently acknowledge the thoughts, take a deep breath, and return your attention to the colors that you see.

After the allotted time (one to five minutes), have a conversation with your students using these questions:

- **What did you notice from that experience?**
- **What was it like to intentionally look at and notice colors in your surroundings?**
- **What different colors did you notice?**

Continue the discussion as time allows.

WEDNESDAY

Objective: To encourage students to be aware of their surroundings and practice being in the moment.

- These exercises can be done while seated, standing, or walking from one place to another.
- If using them during transition, try asking the questions at a stopping point along the way or when you reach your destination.

Today for mindful seeing, we are going to focus on noticing shapes in our surroundings in the present moment. Mindful seeing is a great strategy to help you when you feel like you might need some calm.

Turn your attention to the sights around you. What shapes do you notice? Silently acknowledge the different shapes that you see. If other thoughts arise, gently acknowledge the thoughts, take a deep breath, and return your attention to the shapes that you see.

After the allotted time (one to five minutes), have a conversation with your students using these questions:

- **What did you notice from that experience?**
- **What was it like to intentionally look at and notice shapes in your surroundings?**
- **What different shapes did you notice?**

Continue the discussion as time allows.

THURSDAY

Objective: To encourage students to be aware of their surroundings and practice being in the moment.

- These exercises can be done while seated, standing, or walking from one place to another.
- If using them during transition, try asking the questions at a stopping point along the way or when you reach your destination.

> **Today for mindful seeing, we are going to focus on noticing sizes of objects in our surroundings in the present moment. Mindful seeing is a great strategy to help you when you feel like you might need some calm.**

> **Turn your attention to the sizes of objects around you. What sizes do you notice? Silently acknowledge the different sizes that you see. If other thoughts arise, gently acknowledge the thoughts, take a deep breath, and return your attention to the sizes of objects that you see.**

After the allotted time (one to five minutes), have a conversation with your students using these questions:

- **What did you notice from that experience?**
- **What was it like to intentionally look at and notice different sizes in your surroundings?**
- **What different sizes did you notice?**
- **What similar size objects did you notice?**

Continue the discussion as time allows.

FRIDAY

Objective: To encourage students to be aware of their surroundings and practice being in the moment.

- These exercises can be done while seated, standing, or walking from one place to another.
- If using them during transition, try asking the questions at a stopping point along the way or when you reach your destination.

> **Today for mindful seeing, we are going to focus on noticing our surroundings with our eyes. We don't have to name what we see. We're just going to practice noticing. Mindful seeing is a great strategy to help you when you feel like you might need some calm.**

> **Turn your attention to the sights around you. What do you notice? Silently acknowledge the different and subtle things that you see. There's no need**

to name what you see. Just notice them. If other thoughts arise, gently acknowledge the thoughts, take a deep breath, and return your attention to the things you can see.

After the allotted time (one to five minutes), have a conversation with your students using these questions:

- **What did you notice from that experience?**
- **What was it like to intentionally look at and notice your surroundings?**
- **Did you notice different things?**
- **If so, what was different about the things you saw?**

Continue the discussion as time allows.

MINDFUL EATING SCRIPTS ◆ ◆ ◆ ◆ ◆ ◆ ◆

USE FOR WEEKS 1–36

MONDAY

Objective: To encourage students to slow down and be present with their food.

" **Today for mindful eating, we are going to focus on our sense of smell. The purpose of this exercise is to help us slow down and truly notice our food. Mindful eating is a healthy practice that can help our bodies process our food in a more productive way.**

Start by taking your food and smelling it. What do you notice? Now, take one bite of your food and chew slowly until there is no food left in your mouth. Smell your food again. What do you notice? Has the smell changed at all or is it the same? Take one more mindful bite and chew until there is no food left in your mouth.

Now have a conversation with your students using these questions:

- **What did you notice from that experience?**
- **What was it like to intentionally smell your food?**
- **Did you notice any differences between the first bite and second bite?**

At this point, your students may continue eating and finish their food.

TUESDAY

Objective: To encourage students to slow down and be present with their food.

This exercise involves exploring the sense of touch. Be sure to choose a food cool enough to touch with the fingers and that won't cause too much of a mess.

" **Today for mindful eating, we are going to focus on our sense of touch. The purpose of this exercise is to help us slow down and truly notice our food. Mindful eating is a healthy practice that can help our bodies process our food in a more productive way.**

Take your food and touch it. What do you notice? Now, take one bite of your food and chew until there is no food left in your mouth. Touch your food again. What do you notice? Has the feel changed at all or is it the same? Take one more mindful bite and chew until there is no food left in your mouth.

Now have a conversation with your students using these questions:

- **What did you notice from that experience?**

- **What was it like to intentionally touch your food?**
- **Did you notice any differences between the first bite and second bite?**

At this point, your students can continue eating and finish their food.

WEDNESDAY

Objective: To encourage students to slow down and be present with their food.

Today for mindful eating, we are going to focus on our sense of sight. The purpose of this exercise is to help us slow down and truly notice our food. Mindful eating is a healthy practice that can help our bodies process our food in a more productive way.

Take your food and look at it. What do you notice? Now, take a bite of your food and chew until there is no food left in your mouth. Look at your food again. What do you notice? Has the look changed at all or is it the same? Take one more mindful bite and chew until there is no food left in your mouth.

Now have a conversation with your students using these questions:
- **What did you notice from that experience?**
- **What was it like to intentionally look at your food?**
- **Did you notice any differences between the first bite and second bite?**

At this point, your students can continue eating and finish their food.

THURSDAY

Objective: To encourage students to slow down and be present with their food.

Today for mindful eating, we are going to focus on our sense of hearing. The purpose of this exercise is to help us slow down and truly notice our food. Mindful eating is a healthy practice that can help our bodies process our food in a more productive way.

Take a bite of your food and listen as you chew. What do you notice? Now chew that bite until there is no food left in your mouth. Take another bite of your food. What do you notice? Has the sound changed at all or is it the same? Chew until there is no food left in your mouth.

Now have a conversation with your students using these questions:
- **What did you notice from that experience?**
- **What was it like to intentionally listen as you chewed your food?**
- **Did you notice any differences between the first bite and second bite?**

At this point, your students can continue eating and finish their food.

FRIDAY

Objective: To encourage students to slow down and be present with their food.

 Today for mindful eating, we are going to focus on our sense of taste. The purpose of this exercise is to help us slow down and truly notice our food. Mindful eating is a healthy practice that can help our bodies gain more energy from our food.

Take a bite of your food and really focus on the taste. What do you notice? Flavors? Textures? Chew that bite until there is no food left in your mouth. Now, take another bite and focus on the taste again. What do you notice? Flavors? Textures? Has the taste changed at all or is it the same? Chew until there is no food left in your mouth.

Now have a conversation with your students using these questions:
- **What did you notice from that experience?**
- **What was it like to intentionally taste your food?**
- **Did you notice any differences between the first bite and second bite?**

At this point, your students can continue eating and finish their food.

MODIFICATIONS

Occasionally you may need to modify some of the exercises to accommodate students with varying abilities or change things up to add variety. Here are suggestions for modifying some of the existing exercises to meet the needs of your students.

◆ MINDFUL BREATHING

Adding imagery to mindful breathing can be a fun way to help easily distracted minds focus on the task at hand. Substitute one breathing exercise a week with a variation from the following list. Repeat each exercise five to ten times.

Belly Balloon Breathing: With both hands on your belly, pretend there is a balloon in your belly. Inhale slowly through your *nose* to feel the balloon expand, and exhale through your *nose* to feel the balloon deflate.

Candle Breathing: Hold your index finger in front of your mouth and pretend it's a candle. Take a deep breath in through your *nose*, hold for 1-2-3-4, and exhale through your *mouth* to blow out the candle.

Dandelion Breathing: Make a fist and hold it in front of your mouth, and pretend you are holding a dandelion full of seeds. Take a deep breath in through your *nose*, hold for 1-2-3-4, now exhale strongly through your *mouth* to try to blow every dandelion seed off the plant.

Birthday Cake Breathing: Hold both hands in front of your mouth and pretend you are holding your birthday cake. Take a deep breath in through your *nose*, hold for 1-2-3-4, now exhale through your *mouth* to try to blow out all the candles.

Balloon Breathing: Place both hands on top of your head. Take a deep breath in through your *nose* and raise your hands above your head as if you were blowing up a balloon. Now, slowly exhale and bring your hands back down on top of your head.

Blowing Leaves Breathing: Hold your hand with five fingers up in front of your mouth and pretend it's a tree with leaves. Take a deep breath in through your *nose*, hold for 1-2-3-4, now exhale through your *mouth* and blow your leaf fingers around.

Dragon Breathing: Put your hands around your mouth to make a dragon mouth. Take a deep breath in through your *nose*, hold for 1-2-3-4, now exhale strongly through your *mouth* with your best dragon breath.

Lion Breathing: Take a deep breath in through your *nose*, hold it for 1-2-3-4, now exhale strongly through your *mouth* and roar like a lion.

◆ MINDFUL STRETCHING

It's important to remember that everyone is at a different place physically in terms of what they can do. This can change from day to day. Students should do any stretch to the best of their abilities according to how they are feeling that day.

Do half of the pose: Students with mobility concerns can do a modified version of almost any pose, stretching in whatever way they can in an imitation of the pose. For example, child's pose requires kneeling on the ground, bending forward all the way, and stretching arms out over the head. Someone in a wheelchair might just bend forward at the waist as far as he or she can go and reach his or her hands up over the head.

Use a chair: Anyone who has difficulty balancing will find this helpful. Students might hold on to the back of a chair to gain balance. Or, students can sit in a chair and stretch from a sitting position. Mountain top is a great example of a pose that can easily be performed while seated.

Lie on the ground: Many poses are done in a vertical position, but several can also be done while lying flat on the ground and stretching horizontally. The important thing is to stretch the limbs while assuming the shape of the pose. For example, try downward dog while lying down and raising up your arms and legs into a *V*-shape.

INDEX

About the Author

James Butler has been teaching since 2002, mostly in Austin, Texas, in kindergarten and prekindergarten classrooms. He has a B.S. in education and early childhood from Manchester University (Indiana) and an M.Ed. in curriculum and instruction from Grand Canyon University (Arizona). In 2014, he was honored as the Austin ISD Teacher of the Year. Currently, he serves as the SEL mindfulness specialist for the Austin Independent School District.

Mindful Classrooms is currently being used in over 1,000 classrooms throughout the country. His current role allows him to work with students in grades preK–12 as well as staff and parents in Austin ISD. He also travels around the United States to conduct mindfulness seminars, professional development sessions, and workshops.

James lives in Austin, Texas, with his partner Lindsey Wineholt and their adorable Ewok-looking dog named Theo. You can learn more about his work at mindfulclassrooms.com.

Other Great Resources from Free Spirit

Mindfulness In a Jar®
101 Exercises to Help Children
Focus and Calm Their Minds
by James Butler, M.Ed.
For ages 5–9. 101 cards.

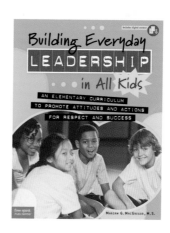

**Building Everyday
Leadership in All Kids**
An Elementary Curriculum to
Promote Attitudes and Actions
for Respect and Success
by Mariam G. MacGregor, M.S.
For teachers, grades K–6.
*208 pp.; PB; 8½" x 11";
includes digital content.*

**Coloring Book and Reflections for
Social Emotional Learning**
by James Butler, M.Ed., illustrated by Becca Borrelli
Available in English and Spanish.
For grades preK–5.
80 pp.; PB; illust.; 6" x 7½".

Mindful Classrooms™ Poster
High gloss, 30" x 19".

EVERYDAY MINDFULNESS SERIES
*by Paul Christelis,
illustrated by Elisa Paganelli*
For ages 5–9.
32 pp.; HC; color illust.; 7½" x 9".
Free Leader's Guide
freespirit.com / leader

Breath by Breath
A Mindfulness Guide
to Feeling Calm

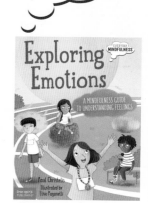

Exploring Emotions
A Mindfulness Guide to
Understanding Feelings

Get Outdoors
A Mindfulness Guide to
Noticing Nature

Sleep Easy
A Mindfulness Guide
to Getting a Good
Night's Sleep

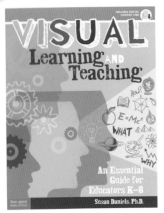

Visual Learning and Teaching
An Essential Guide for Educators K–8
by Susan Daniels, Ph.D.
For educators, grades K–8.
272 pp.; PB; 8½" x 11"; includes digital content.
Free PLC/Book Study Guide freespirit.com/PLC

The Complete Guide to Service Learning
Proven, Practical Ways to Engage Students in Civic Responsibility, Academic Curriculum, & Social Action
(Revised & Updated 2nd Edition)
by Cathryn Berger Kaye, M.A.
For teachers, grades K–12.
288 pp.; PB; 8½" x 11"; includes digital content.

Leadership Is a Life Skill
Preparing Every Student to Lead and Succeed
by Mariam G. MacGregor, M.S.
For administrators and teachers, grades K–12.
168 pp; PB; 7¼" x 9¼"; includes digital content.

The SEL Solution
Integrate Social and Emotional Learning into Your Curriculum and Build a Caring Climate for All
by Jonathan C. Erwin, M.A.
For administrators, teachers, counselors of grades K–12.
200 pp.; PB; 8½" x 11"; includes digital content.

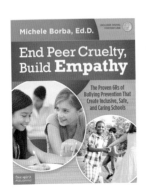

End Peer Cruelty, Build Empathy
The Proven 6Rs of Bullying Prevention That Create Inclusive, Safe, and Caring Schools
by Michele Borba, Ed.D.
For administrators, teachers, counselors, youth leaders, bullying prevention teams, and parents of children in grades K–8.
288 pp; PB; 7¼" x 9¼"; includes digital content.
Free PLC/Book Study Guide freespirit.com/PLC

Character Building Day by Day
180 Quick Read-Alouds for Elementary School and Home
by Anne D. Mather and Louise B. Weldon
For teachers, grades 3–6.
240 pp.; PB; illust.; 6" x 9".

Interested in purchasing multiple quantities and receiving volume discounts?
Contact edsales@freespirit.com or call 1.800.735.7323 and ask for Education Sales.

Many Free Spirit authors are available for speaking engagements, workshops, and keynotes. Contact speakers@freespirit.com or call 1.800.735.7323.

For pricing information, to place an order, or to request a free catalog, contact:

Free Spirit Publishing Inc. • 6325 Sandburg Road, Suite 100 • Minneapolis, MN 55427-3674
toll-free 800.735.7323 • local 612.338.2068 • fax 612.337.5050
help4kids@freespirit.com • freespirit.com